THE ANONYMOUS CHRIST

Jesus as Savior in Modern Theology

LEE E. SNOOK

AUGSBURG Publishing House • Minneapolis

To my children

THE ANONYMOUS CHRIST
Jesus as Savior in Modern Theology

Library of Congress Cataloging-in-Publication Data

Snook, Lee E., 1930–
 THE ANONYMOUS CHRIST.

  Bibliography; p.
  Includes indexes.
  1. Jesus Christ—History of doctrines—20th century.
2. Salvation—History of doctrines—20th century.
I. Title.
BT202.S615   1986   232'.3   86-14117
ISBN 0-8066-2220-2

The paper used in this publication meets the minimum requirements of American National Standard for Information Sciences—Permanence of Paper for Printed Library Materials, ANSI Z39.48-1984.   ∞™

Manufactured in the U.S.A.   APH 10-0370

1   2   3   4   5   6   7   8   9   0   1   2   3   4   5   6   7   8   9

CONTENTS

Salvation and Human Experience
The Constants of Being Human
Lostness as Isolation: Salvation as Reconciliation

Chapter Five: *The Savior as Total Presence and*

Lostness as False Consciousness
Jesus as Total Presence
Salvation as Universal Consciousness
From Christocentrism to Theocentrism
From Particularism to Universality
Jesus as Mediator of Religious Conflict

The Ambiguity of Belief and Betrayal
The Plurality of Secondary Criteria
Plurality and Ultimate Salvation: An Evaluative Summary
The Finality of Christ in the Postmodern Age
The Anonymous Christ
    1. The history and theology of Jesus
    2. The anonymity of Christ

PREFACE

I am greatly indebted to the board, the administration, and the faculty of Luther Northwestern Theological Seminary for the privilege of a sabbatical leave during the academic year 1984–1985. Financial assistance from Lutheran Brotherhood and the Aid Association for Lutherans as well as the Division of Professional Leadership of the Lutheran Church in America was invaluable.

I want especially to thank Dean Gamwell, Professor McGuinn, and the faculty and staff of the Divinity School of the University of Chicago for their hospitality at the Center for the Advanced Study of Religion; and the other fellows of the center for the many hours of conversation as well as their specific responses to a portion of the manuscript for this book. I risk offending other fellows by singling out for special thanks Professor William Dean of Gustavus Adolphus College; our late-night conversations repeatedly forced me to deeper reflection in order to meet his empirical challenges.

President Lesher, Dean Sherman, and Professor Hefner invited me during that same year to be visiting professor at the Lutheran School of Theology at Chicago; their hospitality and the welcome of the faculty made me feel at home in the stimulating environment of Hyde Park. The members of my graduate seminar on Christology at LSTC came from four continents and several of the Chicago Cluster schools. Many of their criticisms and questions have not been adequately met in these pages, but without them the remaining deficiencies of these chapters would be greater in number. Carl Braaten read the entire manuscript at one stage, and, while he has been my harshest critic and I think would not want to be identified with my concluding proposals in Chapter 6, few theologians have given me more encouragement in this effort than he. I want to thank Professor Anne Carr of the University of Chicago for her interest in this project and for criticizing a portion of an early draft and responding to the whole of it near the finish. Two of my New Testament colleagues responded to my request for criticisms of Chapter 1. My thanks to David Tiede for his help and to Arland Hultgren, whose influence as my partner in teaching "Jesus in Scripture and Theology" was an encouragement during the year of our concurrent sabbatical leaves, he in Cambridge, England, I in Chicago. Patrick Keifert read the entire manuscript with obvious care; I have tried to amend my thinking where I agree with his thoughtful judgment and, as a mark of my gratitude to him, look forward to continuing the conversation on those points where we differ.

In addition to her patience with the hectic schedule of our two-career marriage, made more complex by my absence each week, Lois read and reread these pages and helped me repair many inelegant passages. She is innocent of responsibility for those which remain, owing to my incapacity to render a theological point into prose that meets the high standards of speech and writing which she has always exerted in our family.

INTRODUCTION

The Anonymous Christ: Jesus as Savior in Modern Theology is an introduction to contemporary interpretations of Jesus as Savior. As such, its intended readers are students of theology, pastors, teachers of the church, and all persons who have a genuine interest in the importance of Jesus for today. Also, I hope it will be helpful for all those who have difficulty taking the traditional churchly confessions of Jesus as their starting point.

Behind those orthodox creeds about Jesus—as God's only Son who is himself true God and true humanity—there lies an event which centers on Jesus of Nazareth and which is inseparable from the community of believers who wrote the New Testament. That event is deeply transformative in its significance. It purports to mean nothing less than the salvation of the world. This book begins, not with the later formulas about the two natures of Christ, but with that saving event which is *behind* all creeds and speculations about Jesus as the God-man. The final test of any formulation or creed is not whether it accurately repeats the orthodoxies of the past—however helpful they have been or still are—but whether it functions in this day to continue, rather than to hinder, the redemption of the world.

Some theologians are profoundly suspicious of an approach which is, admittedly, a reversal of the traditional sequence of moving from Christology to soteriology. The approach of this book is to proceed from soteriology to Christology. I am convinced that this procedure need not lead to the danger of reducing the Lordship of Christ to the limitations of humans' perceptions of what ails them, cutting

7

God down to human size, making God meet human needs as we perceive them, or fashioning a doctrine of Christ to suit what the marketplace of religious needs demands.

My thesis is that every one of the major Christologies with any currency in the churches today has gained that currency because it is able to show how Jesus saves from the many dimensions of lostness which threaten humanity: idolatrous unbelief, hopelessness, anxiety and alienation, oppression, ecological disaster, isolation, or false and distorted human consciousness. The whole point of Christology from its beginnings in the New Testament until now has been to assert that none other than God can save the world, and that Jesus is God's way of doing just that. No single Christology can contain the final definition of what that means, because the salvation which was definitively and once for all accomplished in Jesus is not yet finished. No Christology from the past, and none today, is a finished, final statement. One of the advantages of reversing the conventional sequence and beginning with Jesus as Savior instead of Jesus as God's only Son is that it opens up the possibility for seeing the many Christologies which are sampled in this book as valid testimonies, even if none of them is the one and only way to honor the truth which Christians confess.

Specialists will quickly note a number of themes and persons who are omitted or relegated to the notes. Rather than include every significant writer, this report has taken another tack: to offer a fairly simple model, consisting of four basic patterns of interpretation, by which to identify and sort out the many interpretations of Jesus. While the argument for the legitimacy of these patterns, based on the New Testament witness and their usefulness for sorting through the multiplicity of modern interpretations of Jesus, is the subject of Chapter 1, several caveats are in order in these introductory pages.

First, each chapter seeks to present the opinions of several authors as clearly and in as strong a light as possible. Of course, no interpretation of Jesus as Savior is beyond criticism but, in the main, critical and evaluative comments have been postponed until the final chapter, when all the perspectives can be related and compared as an aggregate.

Second, in each of the four middle chapters certain theologians are featured. Some of those selected are obvious choices—for example, Barth and Tillich—while others may seem outrageous to some readers—for example, Altizer and Driver. No attempt has been made to include equal numbers of Catholics and Protestants in all sections. One hopes that Catholic readers will not be offended that none of "theirs" appears in one or another category and that Protestant readers will not feel left out that none of "theirs" appears in another. There are a number of references to the work of women and black theologians, but none of them is treated at length. The attempt has been to show how those selected do in fact *illustrate* and *exemplify* a distinctive way of interpreting Jesus today, while recognizing that others could have represented the same point or— some might say—represented it more appropriately. This is not a book of lists with each list completely filled, but it is a proposal for *which* lists to make, and a suggestion for a significant candidate or two with whom to start each list. The author teaches at a Lutheran seminary and has his own preferred—as well as least preferred— Lutheran authors, none of whom appears. The various Christologies of Jürgen Moltmann, Hans Küng, Walter Kasper, Hans von Balthasar, among others, do not receive the attention they deserve. It is a tribute to Moltmann's importance, for example, that, were he to be included, he would appear in several chapters.

Although the following chapters have the flavor of a "survey," their more modest aim is to "sample" modern theologians' assessments of Jesus as Savior.

Third, this book has the didactic purpose of being an "introduction to 20th-century Christology," which indeed could be another subtitle. Novices in theology are therefore reminded that this book is a proposal for getting the "lay of the land." For new arrivals to the theological terrain, here are a map and some tools for analyzing any Christology they might come upon as they wander through bookstalls and library stacks or a seminary curriculum. Needless to say, the great theologians of this century—some of whom appear in this book—have far more to offer than is hinted at in these pages. As already mentioned, those selected have been presented in the strongest possible light, along with suggestions on how to analyze and evaluate their work.

Fourth, there is a slant to this report. As already noted, it is biased toward looking at *all* interpretations of Jesus as biased, and specifically biased in terms of how the interpreter first of all perceives the human predicament for which Jesus as Savior is then interpreted as "Christ." This report tilts toward the view that we know Jesus as Christ in terms of his benefits, which is a dangerous "tilt" because it can lead to making Jesus over into what we think we need. Some of the theologians who appear in this book dispute this bias, and their case against it is presented as fully as possible.

I do not entirely accept George Lindbeck's proposal that Christian doctrines function primarily, if not exclusively, as "rules" for governing theological discourse. (For my disagreement see note 16 in Chapter 1.) I think, however, that his distinction between the "cultural-linguistic" and the "experiential-expressive" view of Christian doctrine can be employed to augment the way I have distinguished present-day Christologies. Lindbeck favors what he calls the "cultural-linguistic" over the "experiential-expressive" because, in his judgment, the task of theology is not to trace doctrine backward to some alleged base in prelinguistic experience. Language, including religious language and doctrine, is transmitted culturally, and any changes in language result from external developments within the cultural-linguistic system, and not from new experiences. The alternative view, of course, is to regard language, and especially faith-language concerning Jesus, as somehow empirically rooted or (I would add) somehow traceable to new historical events (which is to say, transformative events which can be to some degree verified historically). I believe that Lindbeck's twofold distinction can be applied to my fourfold pattern of interpretation:

Chapter	Cultural-Linguistic	Experiential-Historical
2	Barth, Frei	Pannenberg
3	Tillich	Cobb
4	Liberation Theology	Schillebeeckx
5	Altizer	Hick, Rahner, W. C. Smith

Liberation theologians, in particular, are not easily categorized. But I am struck by their confidence in the power of language, especially the language of freedom, which, when linked with the teachings and ministry of Jesus, gives divine authorization for liberating action in the civil order. In fact, they are very careful not to derive their Christologies from the experience of oppression itself but assert that only after one has been immersed in the oppressive situation can one fully understand the meaning of the Jesus story, a meaning which has been there in the text all along, but which privileged Christians have refused to see.

In the final chapter I offer an evaluation of the several approaches to understanding Jesus, and there I also make my own argument for the soteriological bias under the heading *The Anonymous Christ*.

Chapter One

JESUS AS SAVIOR AND THE MANY DIMENSIONS OF LOSTNESS

Three Basic Questions

From the beginning there has been disagreement, even bitter controversy, about Jesus of Nazareth. His career, as reported in the Gospels, was marked by opposition. Even his disciples resisted him. Most notable of all, his death by execution was the result of disputes among civil and religious authorities, disputes which Jesus himself provoked by his public actions and utterances. Arguments about him have often been most intense among those who are devoted to him as Lord. In our own century the wide variety of interpretations—by preachers, philosophers of religion, and professional theologians—of the person and work of Jesus (technically, the theories or doctrines of Christology and soteriology) is positively bewildering. This book will attempt to sort out these often conflicting interpretations by centering on the theme "Jesus as Savior."

Religions, including Christianity, are almost by definition ways of salvation. But there is little agreement among them about what salvation means.[1] Many humanists, for example, would prefer not to speak at all of "salvation" from the human predicament, but of

13

"fulfillment"; others would speak of release, or of enlightenment, or of the ultimate meaning and purpose of life.

We have observed that contemporary theology, especially its many interpretations of Jesus, is a bewildering territory. If we are to draw a map to guide our way, we must keep in mind three questions, all of which are essential to the language of Christian faith, and none of which can be satisfactorily answered in isolation from the others.

Who was Jesus? (the question of Christ's *person*).
What is salvation? (the question of Christ's *work*).
What fact gave rise to these questions?

One might take the view that if only Christians were clear about who Jesus the Christ was and is, and were never to waver in their submission to orthodox dogma, then there could be no confusion or mistake about what salvation means. Some of the theologians dealt with in the following chapters dissent from this view, not least the liberation theologians, who see such a view as an evasion of the political, social, and economic dimensions of salvation. When the first question, Christology (the person of Jesus as the Christ), takes absolute precedence over the second question, soteriology (the work of Jesus as the Christ), it encourages church authorities to limit salvation to allegedly nonpolitical and strictly spiritual activity, and thus to give passive support to oppression.

On the other hand, one might take the opposing view, that if only church leaders and theologians would make Jesus more relevant to the day-to-day needs of ordinary people, then Christianity could get rid of its outmoded dogma and make a difference in real life. Other theologians who appear in the following chapters dissent from such opinions and lodge their protests against allowing our perceptions of psychological desire or our schemes for social reform to control or determine the reality of Christ. For example, at least in the United States, Jesus seems to have been given a new image by market researchers to serve the financially successful "ministry" of the "electronic church," a ministry which has been described as religious entertainment and pop self-help psychology in which one never hears a prophetic word against the status quo.

The phrase *Jesus as Savior* has been deliberately chosen as a way of holding tightly together the three unavoidable questions of Christian faith (Who was Jesus? What is salvation? and What fact gave rise to these theoretical questions?) so that none is given absolute priority over the others. Inasmuch as none of these questions can be answered in isolation from the others, variations or emphases in one will affect and be affected by variations and emphases in the others. The middle four chapters offer ample evidence of the connection and mutual influence among these questions in the work of present-day theologians.

It is generally recognized that after the Council of Chalcedon (A.D. 451) there was a greater consensus among theologians about the person of Jesus as the Christ than about the saving work of Jesus as the Christ. Although there have been controversies aplenty on both counts, and although all theologians would likely agree that the question Who was Jesus? can never be separated from the question What is salvation? it is quite common for textbooks and lectures on Christian doctrine to begin with the first question quite independently of the second. Though probably orthodox, this tactic is no longer suitable and for several reasons.

First, as this book will document, there is in this century no longer a consensus among theologians about the person of Christ. The cultural supports for such a consensus—a legacy from the age of Constantinian Christendom—have collapsed. In a culturally pluralistic context one can no longer take for granted that the classical words upon which the sense and reference of Christological formulations depend have an agreed-upon public meaning anymore, e.g. *God, divine, substance, human, being, essence, person, nature.* How can a Christ whose meaning is obscure at best and simply incomprehensible at worst determine the meaning of salvation—or for that matter even be understood and received as good news?

Second, there is no theological consensus about what, if anything, the words *Savior* or *salvation* can mean in a pluralistic age. It has become obvious to more and more Christians as they encounter other religions through travel, urban neighbors, or college courses on world religions that Jesus is not the only Savior being offered to humanity even if Jesus is the only Savior that most Christians until now have ever known.

Third, as already suggested, even as the explicit church-centered meaning of salvation loses credibility for many, if not most, people of this generation, they are very sensitive to the question of survival of the human race. Nuclear annihilation, mass starvation, ecological disaster, racial hatred, and religious and tribal warfare daily threaten the future of the earth and the earth's most gifted inhabitants, human beings. Because humanity not only has the ability but perhaps also the tendency to bring doom upon all living creatures on earth, there is a new openness to the question of salvation. Salvation is more and more a common, "secular" term, used regularly in politics, athletics, economics, and international affairs. The great question for Christians to think about is whether and how that openness can be linked convincingly and authentically with faith in Jesus as Savior.

Finally, all theologians today recognize that one cannot simply jump into the theoretical issues of Christology and soteriology without at the same time asking the historical question. What happened historically, what new facts emerged, that these doctrinal or theoretical questions have the urgency that they do? Here, too, as we shall see, theologians will disagree. Some will try to finesse the historical question altogether, while others will emphasize the historicity of the cross or the factual character of the resurrection. But none can avoid the issue that fact and theory are tightly related in all modern interpretations of Jesus. This opening chapter proposes that the doctrines and theories about the person and the work of Jesus as the Christ (questions one and two) would never have arisen unless something happened, some originating fact centering on Jesus (question three). I will refer to that originating fact as "the experienced fact of Jesus as Savior" and will try to make clear both its meaning and importance for exploring the terrain of 20th-century theologies.

Although orthodox formulations still guide theological reflection, and Scripture continues to tie new Christologies to the apostolic witness, they are not easily translated into language and action appropriate to the present age. In spite of good intentions and careful scholarship, theology itself seems to be an obstacle to faith in Jesus as Savior.

Theologies: Obstacles to Faith in Jesus as Savior?

Theologians in recent years have been prolific in their production of new Christologies as well as new defenses of old Christologies.

What is required of them is to fashion a Christological vessel fit for the treasure, that is, for the reality of salvation in Jesus. In effect, every preacher and teacher, every Christian who witnesses to Jesus as Savior attempts the same thing: fashioning interpretive wineskins fit for the always new wine, lest by some carelessness or neglect the wine of salvation is not available to the world. Equally at risk, and yet unavoidable, is the possibility that theology, as an obsolete vessel, can itself be the obstacle or hindrance which withholds or obscures the treasure of salvation from those for whom salvation is intended. It is ironic, surely, that those who construct and/or defend Christologies in order that Jesus as Savior might be honored and handed over or transmitted might in fact betray what they intend to revere. The irony is expressed in the word *tradition* itself, whose root meaning is "to hand over." In English as well as in Greek, "to hand over" is ambiguous.[2] With the best of intentions, our efforts to hand over the truth to the next generation may have the effect of betraying the truth to the enemy of truth. Yet the irony that defenders of tradition can in practice be unwitting betrayers is an insight into the dialectic of Jesus as Savior. Jesus as Savior is the point which Christian theology tries to make. Christology is the means for making the point, but is not itself the point. No one is saved—to the extent that anyone is saved—by subscription to a given Christology. Only the fact of a Savior can save, a fact which like all facts is dependent on theories (in this case Christology), but never replaced by them. Everything else, especially including Christology, should have as its point to make and defend that point.[3]

Traditional Christological formulations are widely challenged today as being genuine obstacles to faith, if not in practice betrayals of faith. The challenges are of at least three sorts.

1. Conceptual or rational incoherence

It is no novelty when Christian doctrines or modes of thought are dismissed as irrational, incoherent, or conceptually confusing. The central dogmas of the church have always been susceptible to such attack, perhaps most conspicuously the dogmas of the Trinity and the Incarnation. In the absence of adequately articulated dogmas, faith in Jesus as Savior could not have been transmitted from generation to generation. In any case Christian *believers* are also *thinkers* and *knowers* who, for their own clarity of mind and intellectual integrity, if for no other reason, will seek some connection between their confession of faith and their taken-for-granted conception of reality. These latter conceptions are various, of course, and like maps are always being revised and redrawn from time to time and from place to place.

Most European and North American Christians have been immersed for several centuries in a cultural milieu profoundly influenced by Western science, technology, and the pragmatic methods of a market system economy. It is incorrect to suppose that science, technology, and business are simple and unambiguous systems or that they refer to a fixed set of assumptions and procedures which are never questioned from within; nevertheless, some features of this cultural milieu are so steeped in science and technology that they can be considered widely shared cultural commitments, or what David Tracy has called "faith in the modern experiment."[4] For example, this secular faith embraces openness. In principle, no scientific method or model or conclusion is final or closed to challenge and possible revision. All theories are relatively open to revision; none is beyond criticism. In addition, this faith in the modern experiment entails a view of ultimate reality which extends beyond the specifics of any local experiment. Einstein is often quoted as saying that "the physicist is possessed of a sense of infinite causation." Whether causation is to be conceived as a complex universal machine or as a vast living organism, the commitment here is to a universe in which causal connectedness holds sway and never takes a holiday.

Most educated and thoughtful persons in the West live their lives as though they too shared a commitment to the modern experiment. Even when they believe in miracles as unexplainable interruptions or as exceptions to the causal network, they continue to rely on scientific medicine for their own health, and on sound technology for transportation, for communication, and for food production. They typically live as though causal connectedness were taken for granted; it is their day-by-day practical religion.

Anyone whose mind honors an open and pragmatic, rather than a closed and dogmatic, approach to knowledge, and whose sense of reality presupposes the virtual elimination of all but "natural" causes and "historical" influences will readily acknowledge the challenge to Christology implicit in a pragmatic approach to knowing. How can Christology be regarded, then, as a closed subject? And how can the God-man be rendered conceptually coherent without thinking of Jesus as some kind of absolute exception to the structures of what makes a human human? Conversely, what concepts can we use for thinking of Jesus that will not undermine all that is implied by Jesus as Savior come from God and yet will be compatible with our taken-for-granted notions of reality, notions so heavily influenced by the pragmatic methods of science and technology? Theologians today are working to resolve the apparent conflict between their own taken-for-granted sense for reality as that sense has been shaped by modernity and their commitment to the Christian tradition as true. A major issue is the question of how to formulate interpretations of Jesus as Savior so that they will be not only conceptually coherent but also compatible with modern biblical scholarship.

2. Historical and personal distance

When Christians affirm the experienced fact of Jesus as Savior, they are committed by that affirmation to at least two propositions: *(a)* that in the life and death of Jesus a real saving act took place at a specific time and place, and *(b)* that this salvation in Jesus continues to the present time and will be victorious in some ultimate way at the End. For Christians the historical guarantee of the present and promised salvation was given when God raised Jesus from the dead. Faith in Jesus as Savior seems to be no more secure than one's own historical knowledge, or historical skepticism, about the life, death, and resurrection of Jesus.

Just as conceptions of reality that are informed by positivistic science collide with Christological implications of Jesus as the God-man, historical skepticism has collided with naive ways of presenting Jesus as historical. A "naive" view of what constitutes history has been mostly replaced by a more positivistic or "historicistic" view which is analogous to the scientific view of infinite causation. One version of a naive view of history holds that all events occur just as they do because they are caused or willed by God in a more or less direct way. Even if God should use indirect means to bring about events (through such contingencies as floods or big fish or political powers like Cyrus or Caesar) there is nothing *ultimately* contingent about the events because they could not have occurred otherwise unless God had so willed. That naive view of history has been challenged, and by some replaced, by being relativized as only one possible view of history, but not necessarily the only true one. The naive view is but one idea in the history of ideas *about* history, and the very origin of this naive view (as one of several views) can itself be "explained" by showing how it originated in some cultural or psychological need for reassurance in the face of history's contingencies. The naive view that God is in control of history is an escape from the terrifying prospect that humans are totally at the mercy of accidental or whimsical forces. In the face of personal death or political defeat or natural disaster, it is "natural" for human beings in their naivete—so runs the historicistic challenge—to erect "sacred canopies" of religious beliefs above their precarious personal and social existence and thus to ward off threats of meaninglessness which indeed the "natural" events of death, defeat, illness, and disappointment pose for every human being.[5]

Historicism, skeptical about anything other than historical explanations, has rightly been perceived as a challenge to Christian claims about Jesus as Savior. Generations of theologians have been provoked to rethink what faith in Jesus can mean historically. Here, too, the rethinking risks betrayal—through a new interpretation— of what one is trying to defend.[6]

The mountain of theological books written on this question is ample evidence of the extent to which historical consciousness has dominated theological minds in this century. All who would claim that Jesus is Savior even now, even here, are obliged to frame some judgment about how the seemingly threatening sense of historical distance between the Jesus of the past and existence today can be overcome. That obligation is no less daunting than the challenge raised by scientific worldviews.

3. Moral and religious offense

Historical consciousness for present-day Western Christians does not allow them to ignore two other factors: the moral ambiguity of Christianity throughout history and the variety of other major religious traditions whose devotees share this finite earth with them.

Thoughtful Christians, Jews, Hindus, Muslims, or Buddhists would not likely use the history of their religion as strong evidence for the moral worth of their particular tradition. Religion, as one philosopher has observed, is often a synonym for hatred. That has surely been as much the case in the past as it is today. Christians apparently have often found it very easy to be cruel to one another in the name of Jesus, and especially hostile to persons of different religious traditions or different cultural, racial, ethnic, economic, or political groups. Whenever religion is a factor in any conflict, the possibilities for mutual destruction and for wanton, vicious attacks on the perceived adversary seem to have no limit.

No Christian can evade the historical fact that the New Testament has been interpreted—and thus Jesus has been interpreted—in ways that have permitted and sometimes encouraged the repression and persecution of Jews, the subjugation and humiliation of women, and the enslavement and disenfranchisement of blacks, Orientals, and other racial groups—all in the name of Jesus.[7] No particular tradition within the history of Christianity is innocent of some version of cruelty in the name of Jesus, with the possible exception of the Society of Friends who, ironically enough, are often viewed as outside the stream of Christian history.

Moral consciousness is not only offended by the cruelty and hatred practiced by Christianity in human history, but also by the ways some Christians in the name of Jesus have behaved in relation to other religions. All religious traditions know a saving reality even if the words *savior, redemption,* and *salvation* are not part of their standard vocabulary. What they do not necessarily know, of course, is the experienced fact of *Jesus* as Savior. They might be totally unaware of the history of Jesus as Savior, unless they have come into contact with the Christian missionary enterprise, but they are not necessarily totally ignorant of salvation. Many Christians have been unclear on this point, just as it not uncommon for some theologians to be *very* clear in their insistence that there is absolutely nothing analogous to salvation in the tradition of Jews or Hindus or Muslims or Buddhists. For a Christian to acknowledge the historically verifiable fact that other religious traditions do indeed know some saving reality, or its relative equivalent expressed in terms peculiar to this or that tradition, does not at all deny what is absolutely at the center of the Christian's faith, namely, another fact: the experienced fact of Jesus as Savior. As *facts,* the two are not contradictory. In Chapter 5 we will examine the challenge of some theologians who contend that there is a tragic and needless contradiction in traditional soteriological and Christological *doctrine*. They argue that this contradiction can be removed without diminishing the uniqueness of Christ. For them the needless offense in much Christian theology and practice is analogous to an allegedly democratic society trying to make the point that participatory democracy is the best means of achieving a just and open society, all the while using as a means for making that point policies which in practice make it impossible for many of its own citizens to experience as a fact what democracy is.

The experienced fact of Jesus as Savior is what both doctrines, soteriology and Christology, are about and that from which they flow, even as that fact is also the source of the New Testament writings. All attempts to revise Christian formulations about Christ's person and work are accountable to that fact; they will be judged according to the criterion of whether they make that fact available to all human beings—male and female, Jew and Greek, religious and nonreligious—in order that Jesus, when "handed over," is not, in effect, betrayed.

There would have been no gospel writing or other apostolic witness if Jesus of Nazareth, who was crucified under Pontius Pilate, had not been experienced and confessed as Savior. Early witnesses had experienced an event so compellingly important that they could not remain silent. That experienced event was their salvation accomplished for them in the life and death of Jesus, who was present with them as Lord only because—they were convinced of this—he had been raised from the dead. All attempts in the New Testament to state or describe who Jesus is (the several Christologies of the New Testament and the numerous titles ascribed to Jesus[8]) are predicated on the experience of what Jesus had done, or on what had been accomplished for them through him.[9] The logic is fairly straightforward and familiar. It is only *after* some startling deed for good or ill has been accomplished, whether in politics or sports or the arts or science, that one asks, Who *was* that person? Where did she come from? What or who is the source of his authority? Who or what can account for that power?[10]

One Savior, Many Theologies

Christians have always been more or less united in their faith in Jesus as Savior. They have rarely been united in their understanding of what that faith means. It has been slowly dawning on Christian theologians that unity in *understanding* is probably impossible, but that the diversity of understandings can itself be more easily understood by paying attention to the sources of that diversity, namely, the complex reality of the experience of Jesus as Savior, a reality which is not unambiguously accessible at the end of the 20th century.

It has been nearly 2000 years since anyone has had direct contact with Jesus of Nazareth. Even contemporary Christians who have privileged mystical experiences of being with Jesus do not have that privilege in isolation from prior acquaintance with the Bible or the church or parents or teachers. A mystical union with Jesus will always be union with the one who was first encountered through the tradition; that is, Jesus first comes in mediated ways. This was true even for St. Paul, who did not meet Jesus for the first time when he encountered the resurrected Christ. Prior to his conversion Paul had encountered the reality of Jesus through the preaching and the testimony of Christians whom he had been persecuting. Mystical experiences of Jesus, although intensely personal and interior to the experiencer, do not happen independently of the mediating tradition, without which Jesus cannot be known.

Jesus as Savior has been transmitted by historical means, that is by the Christian tradition: Scripture, creeds, liturgies, confessional writings, homilies, parents, and teachers. So long as this tradition's authority was generally accepted, and so long as the tradition was regarded as relatively unambiguous and trustworthy, there were no pressing reasons to doubt that the Jesus who was presented to successive generations through the historical witnesses was the authentic Jesus. The last several generations, however, have been a time of steady erosion of confidence in those traditional means by which the Jesus story has been handed over from generation to generation. For most Protestants, of course, the difficulty has centered on the Bible, the reliability of which as a historically accurate account has come under attack ever since the Enlightenment. Historical criticism of Scripture, in turn, has stimulated many generations of scholars to find ways for reestablishing the authority of the Bible as a basis for believing in Jesus.[11]

It has become a commonplace among thoughtful Christians to acknowledge that no one any longer has access to a bare, uninterpreted, direct, immediate contact with Jesus, and that all experiences of the real presence of Jesus are themselves dependent upon the social and historical factors which make up tradition. It is not only subjective or mystical experiences of Jesus that are dependent on the historical means by which the Jesus story was first introduced into the mystics' awareness, but also every so-called objective and balanced account of Jesus—most often by scholars trained in the critical-historical methods—is likewise influenced by a multitude of social, cultural, and philosophical factors which the scholars bring to their investigation.

The historical ambiguity of all aspects of the tradition has provoked both fundamentalist responses at one extreme and agnostic responses at the other. Both extremes are similar in this respect: they require solid, unambiguous grounds for religious commitment. The agnostic thus finds faith in Jesus difficult, if not impossible (because there simply are no unambiguous historical grounds for faith), while the fundamentalist must deny the historical (and therefore ambiguous) nature of the tradition in order to believe. Between those for whom historical consciousness has made faith in Jesus impossible and those for whom historical factors are at best simply irrelevant for faith or at worst denied by faith is the wide range of Christians who are both somehow committed to Jesus as Savior and who are also convinced that historical thinking about Jesus is inescapable and appropriate. Intellectual honesty compels them to investigate those sources historically. Theologians in the broad middle of the whole spectrum of theology, when they turn to consider Jesus as Savior, can properly be called revisionists in their Christologies. Revision is the strategy for dealing with the ambiguity without resorting to intellectual double-talk or intellectual schizophrenia.[12]

Jesus has never told his own story and does not tell his own story now. It is a story which does not tell itself; therefore every account of the Jesus story is also an interpretation, a retelling. This is no less true for the several New Testament accounts of Jesus than for any present-day reader of the Christian Scriptures.[13] Every reader of the New Testament encounters in the texts a variety of interpretations of Jesus, whether it is at the level of a "source" or at the level of the final redactor who, guided by certain theological interests, used the received sources in order to re-present Jesus in the light of that theological purpose. In addition, every subsequent generation of New Testament readers and interpreters has been inescapably influenced by the history of interpretation up to its time. That long history of the church's use of Scripture is also a history of biases, a fact which recent historians have called to our attention by uncovering the way certain interpretations of the Jesus story have protected, reenforced, and sanctioned anti-Semitism, sexism, and social elitism within the church. Only by revising the prevailing interpretations of Jesus can the hurt inflicted upon Jews, women, blacks, and others be reduced.[14]

Present-day theologians have not usually given their primary attention to understanding Jesus as Savior.[15] By far the greatest amount of scholarly attention has been dedicated to establishing either reliable historical rootedness (the quests for the "historical Jesus") or a rational defense of the claims of faith (as in the "myth of the incarnation" debate). Only after responding to modern historical skepticism (our third question) and after meeting challenges to the intelligibility of speaking of the divine-human person (our first question) have they taken up the question of Jesus as Savior.

Jesus as Savior: Fact and Theory

Both soteriology and Christology, necessary and inescapable as they are for reflecting on Jesus, have the status more of theory than of fact. The relation between the two is akin to the well-known requirement in the physics of light that there be two theoretical models for understanding what we naively experience as light. The two theoretical models not only require each other in complementary, yet paradoxical ways but also refer to the phenomenon of light for which they are mental constructs by which to explain what is experienced as the fact called light. No one actually sees by virtue of a *theory* of light and indeed one can see quite well, if blessed by good vision, in total ignorance of sophisticated theories. In like manner, soteriology and Christology are related to each other as interdependent theories, but they also refer to a prior fact. Thus:

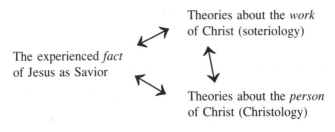

Theories about the *work* of Christ (soteriology)

The experienced *fact* of Jesus as Savior

Theories about the *person* of Christ (Christology)

This simple diagram makes explicit that, as complementary theories, both soteriology and Christology require each other but do not, without remainder, refer back and forth to each other alone. They mutually imply each other but also refer to the prior experienced fact of Jesus as Savior,[16] a fact assumed by both soteriology and Christology. The experienced fact of Jesus as Savior is dependent on suitable theories in order that it be safeguarded from distortion or misuse; that is, if misrepresented by distortion or heresy, the experienced fact of Jesus as Savior could conceivably be inaccessible—simply not available for experience. What theology is obliged to do when reflecting on soteriology and Christology is to safeguard the re-presentation of the experienced fact of Jesus as Savior. Soteriology and Christology do have the status of theory and not of experienced fact, but they are no less important for that. Hence the "arrows" of influence between fact and the two sets of theories flow in both directions.

As a crucial phrase, "the experienced fact of Jesus as Savior" will doubtless strike many New Testament exegetes as an arbitrary choice from among many titles which the Christian Scriptures ascribe to Jesus of Nazareth. On strictly exegetical grounds it is improbable that any one title can be representative for all titles in their various settings and according to their multiple uses. On the other hand, the word *soter* (Savior) scarcely has a narrow, unambiguous meaning or reference as do the terms *centurion, tentmaker,* or *sailor,* for example. Although the term *Savior* is rarely used in the New Testament as a title for Jesus, it has here been adopted deliberately for systematic purposes. The work of Jesus, in the New Testament, is doubtless that of the Savior, and when that term, for systematic purposes, is then expanded into the phrase "the experienced fact of Jesus as Savior" it ascends to the status of such phrases as these:

- the experienced fact of the Exodus as the birth of Israel, the chosen people;
- the experienced fact of the Revolutionary War as the establishment of political independence;
- the experienced fact of the Civil War as the preservation of the Union;
- the experienced fact of N. as my father.

What these illustrative phrases underscore is that *significant experienced facts are never mere isolated instants* snatched from the flow of experience nor bare uninterpreted events which could have been reported with complete objectivity by some mechanical device such as a camera (again see note 16). Any adequate report of an experienced fact will always have a narrative quality to it. This is quite clear in the courtroom proceedings of a trial when the several parties involved seek a judgment about the "facts." Similarly, no single moment, no isolated "slice" of the story of Jesus as variously presented by the New Testament writers, can be identified exclusively as the most important—requiring none of the others—for giving us the straight facts. Nor does any of the episodes in the Jesus narrative present him in absolute isolation. From birth to death Jesus is always seen in relationships with those who interact with him. When he prays alone, he does not pray to himself. Even when he is in the wilderness Jesus cannot be totally alone. The story of Jesus is never the story of Jesus only, nor is it the story "as told by" Jesus only. The experienced fact of Jesus, then, is a narrative of interactions which do not end, not even at the conclusion of the canonical Gospels.[17]

The experienced fact of Jesus also includes *how* he was experienced, principally but not exclusively as Savior. There is more than one experienced fact of Jesus. Even the New Testament makes it clear that there was also, for instance, the experienced fact of Jesus as blasphemer, or the experienced fact of Jesus as sinner. It is a fact that Jesus ate with sinners and it is a fact that he therefore was experienced as a sinner. There has never been unanimity in the way people experienced Jesus, or even in how they referred to him. *Savior,* however, is one of the New Testament terms which can be

reasonably put forth as compatible with others of the apostolic tradition. It has the advantage for systematic purposes of being inclusive in that sense as well as functional. Admittedly, the terms *Messiah, Redeemer, Lord,* or a number of others might have been
selected. The argument here is that Jesus, even before he was crucified, was in some sense experienced as the bringer, embodiment,
teacher, or preacher of good news from God.[18] But if, prior to the
crucifixion, Jesus had *not* been experienced as in *some sense* good
news come from God, it makes no sense that he attracted a sufficiently large following to have been perceived as a threat and a
"blasphemer" and thus to have set in motion those events which
led to his crucifixion. Without followers who in some sense had
experienced Jesus as Savior, he would not have been a political and
religious nuisance—let alone a serious threat to the civil and cultic
establishment. The fact is that he *was* experienced as some kind of
authority who challenged the civil and cultic establishments; otherwise his crucifixion, if it had happened at all, would have been
scarcely noticed.

Similarly, the experienced fact of Jesus as raised from the dead
would scarcely have been reported if there had been no one to make
mention of it. The *historical* value or weight of the resurrection of
Jesus cannot be measured independently of the testimony of those
who witnessed his appearing to them. If Jesus had been raised from
the dead in total isolation, and had appeared to no one, that would
have been the end of it simply because it would not have been
accessible as an experienced fact. There would have been no fact
called resurrection to talk about.[19]

Experienced facts are the only facts available. But experienced
facts are also always relative *qua* experienced facts. In the absence
of an adequate theory (or doctrine), the relativity of all experienced
facts makes them easily misunderstood, misused, distorted, and
completely vulnerable to repudiation. In the absence of an adequate
Christology the experienced fact of Jesus as Savior does not yet have
the status of a truth claim or of universal significance by which to
guide one's life. Nevertheless,

(1) it is a fact *that* Jesus was and is experienced as Savior, and
(2) it is also a fact that *what* the experienced fact of Jesus as
    Savior entails is the relatedness of the Savior with the saved,

of the event of salvation with the experience of those who are saved. Jesus may alone save, but Jesus all alone would be no Savior.[20]

These facts do not alone establish their truthfulness, nor do they, as facts, make explicit claims for themselves. The making and the defending of claims of truthfulness, relevance, and reliability are what soteriology and Christology are all about: the mind of faith seeking to order the facts of faith in theories or doctrines which will be adequate carriers, defenders, and interpreters of the experienced fact of Jesus as Savior.

In the history of reflection on Jesus as Savior, Christological theory eventually hardened into the dogmatic formula of Chalcedon (A.D. 451). Modern theology has repeatedly paid homage to this formula for successfully beating down the several heresies which were serious threats to the core faith of Christianity centered on the experienced fact of Jesus as Savior. Some theologians have also repeatedly criticized the formula for its conceptual inadequacy, or at least for the tendency to make the formula *itself* the sole measure of faith. Soteriology, on the other hand, has exhibited a continuing resistance to a hardened dogmatic formulation or a single authoritative image or metaphor at all analogous to the "two natures" language of Chalcedon.

Soteriology has never been given a finished definition. There is no soteriological dogma.[21] Whatever historical occasions may have prompted the formulation of dogmas about the person of Christ, they are clearly the answer to the prior question, How is salvation through Jesus to be understood as somehow grounded in what is ultimate, lasting, or transcendent? How can the experienced fact of Jesus as Savior be itself saved from relativism, illusion, and dismissal as a mere passing episode in history? What is it about this *person* which prevents what he *did* from being insubstantial or of no everlasting importance? What constitutes this person, Jesus, so that the experienced fact of him as Savior is securely grounded?[22]

The same experienced fact drives the mind of faith in the direction of theorizing about salvation. Here the subject is not primarily the identity and the unity of the person of Jesus as Savior who is, after all, one and only one *person*. The subject of soteriology is an action, an event, a deed, with more than one actor. God, Jesus as Savior, the devil, and all humanity are depicted as actors in the drama of salvation. There is only one Savior, but the Savior acts among other actors. Salvation is intractably complex because this one person Jesus, as actor, *must* act among other agents if there is to be salvation, but whatever else other agents might be thought to *do* in that drama, their status as agents must not minimize or compromise the all-sufficiency of the salvation wrought by the one Savior. The experienced fact of Jesus as Savior has often been betrayed by a faulty soteriological theory, most commonly as one form or another of Pelagianism. Every theory of the atonement illustrates the difficulty of capturing in a single image or metaphor the saving action of *one* Savior whose saving action is nevertheless and necessarily tied to the agency of others without whose acts there would have been no saving event.[23] A Savior all alone is no Savior. Even Judas' betrayal is caught up in all that was necessary, although woe falls upon him for his betrayal (Luke 22:22).

Soteriology: Dimensions of Lostness

The steady insistence thus far has been that there might be a better chance for understanding the present-day theological ferment about Jesus if one were to keep more clearly in mind the theoretical, and therefore variable, nature of all Christological and soteriological formulations. In other words, a more promising way of exploring the bewildering territory of contemporary theories about Jesus is to focus on the variable but nevertheless experienced fact of Jesus as Savior which, while admittedly a complex fact, is intelligible to the modern sensibility so accustomed to the many dimensions of human experience. A major factor in the irreducible complexity of the central fact of Christianity is the various ways in which human beings experience lostness. How a person of another time and culture would perceive lostness cannot be predicted in advance.[24] Lostness may be universal but it is not uniformly experienced, defined, and/or interpreted. In certain stages of a culture's development, or even in the various passages of one person's life, one or another dimension of lostness will have greater urgency and prominence without necessarily excluding others altogether.

The term *lostness* as a designation of that condition and those actions from which Jesus has come to save is certainly compatible with biblical themes like rebellion, sin, idolatry, and the fall. It includes within its scope such categories as moral failure, transgression, loss, or impairment of the image of God in the human. Whatever or whoever is lost is in need of restoration or of rescue from danger or oblivion. Jesus told familiar stories about lostness: the lost coin, the lost sheep, the lost or prodigal son. In these parables of the kingship of God the one who *seeks* the lost is tireless and steadfast, unwavering in determining to find the lost, but lostness itself as a condition is variously described, and so also are the various strategies for restoring, rescuing, and reconciling the lost. Biblical images of lostness are numerous, to be sure, and they run the gamut of metaphors drawn from nature (threatening storms, floods, rocky soil, withered trees), domestic life (foolish bridesmaids, prodigal and disobedient children), economic order (spiteful workers, unjust stewards, straying sheep), and politics (the apocalyptic kingdom overthrowing all accustomed civil order). The reality and the threat of lostness are depicted in such variety that no systematic ordering can reduce them to a simple statement. Nevertheless, it is possible by means of a theologically based structure to sort out what are here being called dimensions of lostness.

Lostness is a relational term, the negative of the more fundamental positive. Lostness implies that what or who belong together, or belong in a proper relation, are in *dis*relation, are divorced. The relation, though radically damaged, nevertheless persists as a necessary requirement for defining identity in lostness. A marriage, even when broken by divorce, continues as a factor which defines a person as divorced. The dialectic of lostness is that *relationships* never end; they continue as reminders, so to speak, of lostness. Divorce is the negative form of marriage; divorce *is* a relationship that has been transformed by brokenness—but a relationship nonetheless. The relation, though radically damaged, is nevertheless a requirement for describing the condition of brokenness. As a relational term, then, *lostness implies a relation* that has been somehow put out of joint, broken, damaged, fractured, rejected, refused, repudiated, rebelled against, displaced, neglected, forgotten, betrayed, mistreated, abused, sinned against, repressed, misrepresented, impugned, ridiculed, obscured, mocked, and scorned.

Christian theology is that discipline which has as its explicit subject matter an irreducibly tripartite relationship which can be diagrammed very simply in this way:

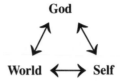

None of the entities or terms thus designated is adequately definable as God or world or self without relating each to the others. Theology is the one discipline which devotes itself explicitly to the *relationship* of the actual world, actual selves, and God.[25]

By now it should be clear that a presupposition for theology today is that no one of these terms by itself or in relation to the others has a universally accepted definition. *How* one speaks of God and world and self is an open question today, but theologians are those for whom it is *not* an option *whether* to speak of God, world, and self. The definitions are open for revision but, what is not open for reconsideration is whether the theologian can turn in the hand that is dealt for a new one. *How* a theologian construes what is dealt will be influenced by many factors that are personal and confessional, historical and cultural. *Whether* one accepts this particular complex subject or not is what determines if one is a theologian.[26]

The structure of theology can easily be seen to have three polarities; that is, the tripartite relation is comprised of three inseparable relations—God and self, God and world, world and self. The dimensions of lostness, therefore, can be sorted out by locating them as distinct disrelations that occur primarily along any one of those three polarities. Lostness as disrelation thus has several dimensions. Disturbances along any one of the three vectors will disturb all three. For example, alienation between self and world (as between me and thee as part of the world) will be between two entities which are not separable from, but are essentially related to God, and thus one can envision that a disturbance between me and thee will also surely disturb the other two polarities, God and self, God and world.

Contemporary Christologies can, without seriously misrepresenting them, be organized according to which sort of disrelation is most emphasized, so that a particular Christology can be characterized according to how the experienced fact of Jesus as Savior is grounded in the experienced fact of lostness.[27]

Chapter 2 will sample several influential Christologies which give primary emphasis to the God-self relation or, more exactly, the God-self disrelation. Thus lostness is the self in rebellion against God. Theologians from Luther to Barth would share this perception of lostness, construing Christ as the Word through whom God wins the self away from the self's rebellion and turns rebellion into faith. Pannenberg, as we shall see, cannot accept the implicit fideism in certain Christologies "from above" and sets out to establish faith firmly on a historically and scientifically credible basis. For Pannenberg, Christ is the End *of* history proleptically revealed *in* history as guaranteed *by* the historically verifiable resurrection.

Chapter 3 takes up the disrelation along the God and world polarity. Many post-Enlightenment worldviews which have captivated the Western mind have no place for God as the necessary, universal causal Agent without whom nothing in the world could live. Even some theologians have yielded all causal explanation of the world to the naturalist philosophers and scientists, but this neglect of the God-world relation tends to close off theological participation in discussions about ecological issues, which are so devastating today. It also tends to undercut the theological warrant for granting to other religions a theological integrity apart from the Christian's knowledge of God through Christ. The second sampling of Christologies, in Chapter 3, is an attempt to repair these deficiencies. Paul Tillich has especially attended to lostness as its effects are noted primarily along the God-world polarity. The fundamental characteristic of the disharmony between God and the creation is the *estrangement* into which even the nonhuman creatures have been drawn because of the hubris, concupiscence, and idolatry of humanity.

When the agenda for Christology is set by lostness defined as disrelation along the God-world polarity, the task is surely daunting, because the reconstruction must occur along many fronts and in conversation with partners of every discipline and religion. The process theologian John B. Cobb Jr. is a prominent figure in these conversations, and his work will be considered as a highly significant contribution to modern understandings of Jesus as Savior.

Chapter 4 deals with Christologies which stress the experience of lostness as the disrelation of self and world. Existential/epistemological as well as aesthetic/cosmological experiences of lostness are regarded by proponents of such Christologies almost as a luxury of elite academic theologians. Lostness as expressed by theologians in Chapter 4 principally takes the form of political oppression, social dislocation, systemic injustice, and economic alienation. Christological proposals by these theologians respond to lostness defined more in ethical and sociological terms. Here the conversation partners are, understandably, political theorists, social philosophers, and—not least—Marxist intellectuals. Again, there are two subtypes. The first of these stresses the political dimension of lostness and so the emphasis is on the problem of freedom and equality. The second focuses on lostness more in terms of the nonperson, of social isolation and polarization; the problem here is one of community and order. Liberation and Marxist theologians belong in the first group, and Edward Schillebeeckx in the second.

We will consider in Chapter 5 those theologians whose challenge is perhaps the most radical of all. To them the problem is that too many interpretations of Jesus reflect what one might call the "Western" or "Latin" captivity of the church. The entire God-self-world schema upon which these interpretations are based must be abandoned because, as Thomas J. J. Altizer argues, it presupposes a dualism in which God the absolutely transcendent is set over against self and world, a dualism which Jesus had to destroy in order to inaugurate the kingdom of God as the kingdom of "total presence." Other thinkers, like John Hick and Wilfred Cantwell Smith, insist that the Western domination of most theological interpretations of Jesus make genuine dialog with non-Western religions impossible. One cannot leave it to Western sensibilities about the God-world-self triad to define what Jesus as Savior must mean to nonwesternized persons. These radical proposals, then, are challenges to the whole thought-structure on which much Christian theology has been built.

The final chapter is a proposal for orchestrating the contributions of all these Christologies, and for seeing them not so much as competitors for dominance in the open market of theology but as many voices or instruments giving testimony to multidimensional truth. A plurality of Christologies does not have to be resolved like a contest among many teams in the big league of Christian theology players, with only one winner and many losers at the end of a tough tournament. The Bible is a far better guide than the sports page for coping with multiple Christologies. No single prophet of Israel is sufficient for understanding "prophecy" and no single apostolic witness of the New Testament for defining "Christ." Even so, there are certain rules or criteria for evaluating the many players in the theological orchestra, and this concluding essay reviews not only the various secondary but also the ultimate criteria by which every Christology must be judged. In the end, I propose that the whole point of reflecting on Jesus as Savior is not only to serve the visible mission which Jesus gave to the church but also to discern Christ as the anonymous giver of salvation regardless of the visible sponsorship under whose auspices the gift is given.

To the degree that any Christology has been persuasive in the Christian communities, that acceptance should rest on its being useful in communicating, clarifying, and making the experienced fact of Jesus as Savior accessible so that this fact may be experienced anew, and by others. A Christology—however orthodox—can sometimes failed to make clear the experienced and experiènceable fact of Jesus as Savior, perhaps most often when it is used forcibly to prescribe and predict rather than to describe and to communicate. Prescriptive and predictive Christologies then can become weapons which—sad to say—theologians use against one another, confirming the suspicion that theologians deserve their reputation of being mean-spirited when dealing with one another. Perhaps one way to lower the level of such animosity is to keep in mind the dimensions of human lostness—so vast and threatening to humanity that no one ought to begrudge the ingenious generosity of God in saving someone else, but instead ought to be grateful that the experience of salvation continues to go beyond all theories and doctrines, and to confound quite a few of them.

Chapter Two

THE SAVIOR
AS THE WORD
AND AS THE END

Sometimes I don't like the word christology very much. It is not a matter of christology, nor even of christo-centricity and a christological orientation, but of *Christ himself.* Any preoccupation with christology . . . can only be a critical help towards coming to the point where we may have the experience of the disciples on the Mount of Transfiguration: "They saw no one but Jesus alone."

This comment by Karl Barth,[1] made in response to someone's description of his theology as a concentration on Christology, is strikingly similar to the conclusion of the previous chapter. If Christology does not describe and communicate the experienced fact of Jesus as Savior, then it fails to do what it is intended to do.

There is no Christian theologian in the 20th century who is more influential than Karl Barth (1886–1968). His reputation and authority would be amply deserved if for no other reason than his mastery of the subject matter. Even the most casual acquaintance with Barth's enormous output of published works will show how thoroughly knowledgeable he was in the history of Christian thought, in Western philosophy, in biblical studies, and certainly in gauging the impact of the Enlightenment on European thought and culture. He was an exacting student of Protestantism's efforts to come to terms with the disciplines of science, philosophy, and history, which had become independent of religious authority after the Reformation and especially during the 18th and 19th centuries. As a student he heard lectures by great theologians who argued that some kind of intellectual partnership should be sustained between theology and other disciplines, that theology and philosophy, faith and reason, Christianity and civilization—indeed Protestantism and German culture— in some important respects needed each other and could be of mutual service to one another. As a village pastor who tried to bring together these two realms in his preaching, he found this theology increasingly impossible as a basis for proclamation. Later he was to say that the Bible is not "man's thoughts about God" (as 19th-century biblical scholars were wont to say) but rather the Bible is "divine thoughts about man." His efforts to follow his teachers' example in correlating Christianity and civilization on the basis of some underlying principle which all reasonable persons should be able to grasp came to ruin as the First World War erupted in Europe in 1914. He later wrote:

> For me personally a day at the beginning of August in that year was the *dies ater* [the black day], when ninety-three German intellectuals published an endorsement of the military policy of Kaiser Wilhelm II and his councillors, on which to my horror I found the names of almost all the theological teachers whom hitherto I had confidently respected. If they could be so mistaken in ethos, I noted that it was quite impossible for me to adhere any longer to their ethics or dogmatics, to their exposition of the Bible or presentation of history. So far as I was concerned, there was no more future for the theology of the 19th century.[2]

It is no exaggeration to say that Karl Barth almost singlehandedly demonstrated in what ways 19th-century theology had failed, and that with his justly famous commentary, *The Epistle to the Romans,* Barth turned the direction of much Protestant theology 180 degrees. The failure of the 19th-century theologians of whom he disapproved was that they tried to establish some other foundation for theology than Jesus Christ. He never tired of insisting that Christian faith is not bound to any human view of reality. "The Christian Confession has in the course of the centuries passed through more than one world-picture. . . . Christian faith is fundamentally free in regard to all world-pictures. . . . As Christians we must not let ourselves be taken captive either by an ancient picture . . . or one newly arisen and beginning to be dominant. And above all we must not combine the Church's business with this or that *Weltanschauung*."[3] His own studies of the disastrous effects of combining the Christian confession of faith with the dominant conceptions of the world convinced him that it all commenced with the greatest of all theologians in the 19th century, Schleiermacher.

"The first place in a history of the theology of the most recent times belongs and will always belong to Schleiermacher, and he has no rival." The 19th century was, in Barth's estimation, "his century." Barth's admiration of Schleiermacher knew no bounds, especially his determination to think dogmatically. What Barth rejected was Schleiermacher's view that

civilization as the triumph of the spirit over nature is the most peculiar work of Christianity, just as the quality of being a Christian is for its own part the crown of a thoroughly civilized consciousness. The kingdom of God . . . is utterly and unequivocally identical with the advance of civilization.[4]

Schleiermacher's devotion to dogmatics as the science of theology was matched by his equal devotion to "modern cultural awareness" as a second loyalty. "He did not only advocate modern civilization, but proclaimed and demanded it." In Barth's opinion, the same teachers who could, as theologians, endorse the military policy of the Kaiser nearly a century after Schleiermacher were merely continuing what Schleiermacher had so brilliantly begun: the identification of the kingdom of God with human civilization. As Barth interpreted Schleiermacher, the two were mutually supportive of each other. Thus, theology was supported by philosophy in terms of a philosophical theology "which was meant to demonstrate that the existence of churches—not the Christian church in particular, nor any particular church—was 'an element necessary to the development of the human mind,' and not by any means an 'aberration.' "[5]

Because of the legacy of Schleiermacher, Christianity and modern European civilization had become—in Barth's view—a very cozy partnership. Christianity, according to the dominant Protestant theology, was necessary to sustain the goals of civilization, and civilization, as interpreted by "modernity," was an essential support for Christianity. This comfortable arrangement was widely endorsed by the liberal theologians with whom Barth had studied, and was the basis on which they had interpreted Scripture and had understood Jesus as the Christ. And when the *dies ater* descended upon Europe there was no Word from God by which theologians or university intellectuals could interpret what was happening. It was as though Jesus as Savior had been silenced by a conspiracy among the liberal theologians who had sincerely believed that indeed it was they who were saving the Christian message from the scorn and disbelief of cultured persons. It was Karl Barth more than any other who allowed the Word to be a saving message again by freeing the Word from those who, in the interest of defending Christianity, had enslaved it.

Barth first earned his reputation as the theologian who, while serving a village parish in Switzerland from 1911 to 1921, used Scripture to turn theology around. From that time on he was a professor of theology, first in Germany and then, after he was exiled by the Nazis in 1935, at Basel in Switzerland. Barth's theology proved itself highly effective in opposing the Nazi regime when he served as a principal author of the Barmen Declaration. This theological document, more than anything else, precipitated his expulsion by the Nazis. In the Barmen Declaration the legacy of liberal Protestantism was most sharply set in contrast to what was later to be called neoorthodoxy. Here the "cultural theology" of the so-called German Christians (*Deutsche Christen*) was opposed by the "crisis theology" of the new "Confessing Church"; here a theology of adaptation was countered with a theology of dissent; here a theology which had been devoted to explanation and apologetics met an opposing theology of proclamation and dogmatics.

In the 19th century, according to Barth, theology had lost its power to communicate the Word of God because theologians had tried to establish its legitimacy or to guarantee its position by accommodating theology to the sciences and worldviews of the century. Thus when the very culture to which theology had adapted itself was sliding toward the disaster of World War I, the so-called cultural theologies were swept along in the avalanche. Later, as Hitler was consolidating his power, Barth's dialectical or crisis theology was the basis for Christian opposition, while other theologians, for example, the Lutherans Werner Elert and Paul Althaus, opposed the Barmen Declaration and countered it with the Ansbach Statement in support of Hitler.[6]

Lostness as Unbelief

In Barth's view, the failure of liberal theology is its unbelief. Rather than being the happy science devoted to the knowledge given in the Word of God, this failed theology devoted and devotes itself to exploring other knowledge in the hope that such other knowledge might provide some clues, some analogies, to what is also given in the Word. For Barth, to accept that procedure is to betray the proper task of theology, because it reveals a fundamental unbelief, a failure to trust the sufficiency of the Word. When theology works in the grip of unbelief it looks elsewhere—to philosophy or science—for assurance that what is given in the Word really can be trusted as knowledge. The presumption of unbelief is that one can somehow pronounce judgment on the Word, whether from the seat of reason, of self-consciousness, or of human experience. As soon as a theologian tries to establish independent grounds for making judgments about the Word, then that theologian has yielded to anxious unbelief which cannot possibly be cured even by the most strenuous appeals to philosophy, psychology, or religious experience.

It is completely unfair to Barth to accuse him of being antirational or antiphilosophical or opposed to explorations of the human consciousness or of the dimensions of experience. There is nothing under the sun in which Barth could not be interested. The fundamental difference between theology and other disciplines—like philosophy—is not one of subject matter, but of method. The philosopher begins from below with reason or experience and perhaps will even move upward toward God, but the theologian begins from above, from the Word, and moves toward human experience and reason. If a theologian should be asked to defend this particular approach "he must answer directly and without qualification, without being ashamed of his naivete, that Jesus Christ is the one and the entire truth through which he is shown how to think and speak, just as strictly as the philosopher is given his task."[7] If a theologian does *not* begin with the truth of Jesus Christ, then that theologian is not so much ignorant or unlearned but simply an unbeliever, that is, he or she does not trust the truth that is given to the joyful science of theology to explore. Lack of faith is not ignorance (which can be cured by correct information) but refusal to live by grace and allow trust in what God has done in Jesus to be the guide for reason and experience. The Word delivers us from *trusting* in reason and experience and instead is the basis for *using* reason and experience. Faith in the Word illuminates reason so that reason, freed from anxiety about proving itself, can understand that faith, rightly understood, *is* reason, that indeed faith is a kind of knowledge, not in the sense of *scientia* or scientific knowledge but in the sense of *sapientia* or wisdom, the practical knowledge by which we can live. "To live by this . . . truth is the meaning of Christian knowledge. Christian knowledge means living in the truth of Jesus Christ. . . . Christian knowledge, at its deepest, is one with what we termed man's trust in God's Word."[8]

Obviously, Barth's insistence that trust in God's Word has priority over all other claims to truth or knowledge does not entail a rejection of whatever can be known through science, history, philosophy, or psychology. It is just that these other forms of knowledge cannot be the basis for what we might here call *saving knowledge*. Philosophy cannot save, psychology cannot save, and history itself is not redemptive. It is folly to put one's trust in that which cannot save, whether it is the Kaiser, Hitler, princes, philosophy, or the multiplication table. All of these can be evaluated and either enjoyed or repudiated from the view of that truth which saves, but none of them can be trusted as that Word which has priority. Nevertheless, when Barth considered those theologians who tried to use human knowledge as a basis for establishing or defending or explaining the truth of Jesus Christ, he could be vehement in denouncing such efforts.[9] Barth was quick to detect what he thought was a mixing together of the knowledge of God which saves with mere human knowledge, in the form of philosophy of religion, for example.

There was no question that for Barth human beings *could* think—and in that sense could know by their own power or understanding or feeling "something like a supreme being, an absolute nature, the idea of an utterly free power, of a being towering over everything." But such a being who can be thought through natural reason cannot be the God who is known only through Jesus Christ. "Man is able to think this being; but he has not thereby thought God. God is thought and known when in His own freedom God makes Himself apprehensible."[10]

God *can* be known, of course, but not on the basis of some natural capacity within the human species, nor because of an underlying structure of existence or being on the basis of which certain analogies can be asserted. Barth regarded all appeals to natural theology or to *analogia entis* as totally invalid bases for the true knowledge of God. God is known only where God has revealed God's own self and this self-revelation "involves the dislodging of man from the estimation of his own freedom."[11] In the presence of God's self-revelation all human efforts to use freedom, reason, experience, etc., to know God are judged. What one is able rationally to conceive as the nature of God is exposed as no god when God is known through God's own revelation. The fundamental distinction here, of course, is between two kinds of knowledge. There is human knowledge as control over certain data, facts, and ideas which then become the object and content of knowledge. This knowledge empowers the human knower to sit in judgment over, and to evaluate, what is known. There is also knowledge as faith or trust given in God's self-revelation. God's revelation of God's own self not only discloses that God is trustworthy but also gives to the receiver of revelation the faith which trusts and knows the revelation as true. By this knowledge the knower/believer is able to trust not only oneself but even one's claims on knowledge of God, the Revealer. The first sort of knowledge (natural theology, general knowledge, clarity of ideas) cannot of itself persuade the one who has such knowledge to trust oneself and all one has—including one's knowledge—into the safe keeping of Another because (if for no other reason) the Other cannot be *known* to be trustworthy until the Other says or does something that reveals the Other to *be* trustworthy. To know another as trustworthy is the equivalent of trusting that one. Such knowledge-as-trust cannot be gained independently of God's self-revelation. The "natural" knowledge one possesses is no more trustworthy than any other human possessions when true knowledge of God is at stake, and for Barth that is exactly what is at stake. Only Jesus is the revelation of God which delivers true knowledge of God, that is the trusting, saving knowledge which both judges and illuminates all other knowledge.[12]

Jesus as the Word

Karl Barth would no doubt be very suspicious of the approach being taken here, namely, distinguishing various Christologies according to the perception of the human predicament which is assumed to lie behind every constructive effort to offer a critical theory of Christ's person and work. His suspicion, one can imagine, is that this approach begins with "man" and moves toward revelation and thus, one more time, a theology is constructed on the basis of an anthropological assumption and not on God's self-revelation. Barth would have been unwilling to *begin* with an analysis of the human condition, because then the human perception—and not the divine revelation—would control all the theological topics. Salvation is a theological, not an anthropological, topic and therefore, even if one were first to acknowledge sin, it would be illegitimate, because it would introduce the question of the *human* condition prior to *divine* revelation as the sole basis of Christian knowledge. To state it boldly, apart from God's self-revelation in Jesus Christ human beings do not really know the truth about their condition. It was part of the failure of 19th-century theologians, especially Ritschl, to suppose that lostness could be defined *before* revelation.[13] The Word of God in Jesus can *save* from lostness only if it first of all *discloses* lostness in its abysmal contrast with the righteousness and grace of God. The entire approach of this book would fall under Barth's criticism for proceeding from an analysis of humankind which then—wrongly—promises to help in comprehending the truth of God's revelation. The theologian does not take the measure of God, but God sets the terms for the theologian's work.

It has already been pointed out that Barth knew exceptionally well the history of all efforts to establish the truth of Christianity with at least the partial help of some prevailing worldview, philosophical system, or interpretation of history. His complaint was that the Christ who emerged from such efforts was not the Christ through whom God established the heavens and the earth and redeemed a lost humanity but was a Christ whom the theologians thought they had saved from obscurity or cultural irrelevance. Such acculturated theology cannot be evangelical theology.

> Ever since the fading of its illusory splendor as a leading academic power during the Middle Ages, theology has taken too many pains to justify its own existence. It has tried too hard, especially in the nineteenth century, to secure for itself at least a small but honorable place in the throne room of general science. This attempt at self-justification has been no help to its own work. . . . Theology had first to renounce all apologetics or external guarantees of its position within the environment of other sciences, for it will always stand on the firmest ground when it simply *acts* according to the law of its own being.[14]

Apart from the revealed Word, in Barth's view, lostness is so total and abysmal that there is within the human situation no capacity for doing theology or for even fashioning a question for which the Word is the answer from God. Theology can only be a response to the Word. It is not an *explanation* of how God has dealt with lostness, but rather serves the *proclamation* of the Word who is Jesus Christ. Theology, then, does not begin with a question, even the question implied by some dimension of lostness, because apart from the prevenient Word any description of lostness can only be based on anthropological categories, which by definition are not theologically derived, that is, not derived from the Word. Theology, in short, does *not* respond to *human* questions which are addressed to it from out of the depths of lostness, but theology *does* respond: "Theology responds to the Word which God has spoken, still speaks, and will speak again in the history of Jesus Christ which fulfills the history of Israel."[15]

Barth is undaunted by any of the alleged problems raised by historical interpretation of the Scriptures. What is essential to the Bible is its witness to the Word, not only the Word as spoken through the prophets, but also as it is incarnate in Jesus Christ and then proclaimed through the apostolic tradition. The Word does not just fall unaided out of the Scriptures; it must be sought. Only when one searches the Scriptures as a theologian—in the sense that Barth has defined that term—will the truth of the Word be found there. "Every possible means must be used: philological and historical criticism and the more remote textual relationships, and not least, the enlistment of every device of the conjectural imagination that is available."[16] Barth is no biblicist. The Bible alone is not sufficient for discernment of the Word of God. Nor is the Bible, apart from appropriate imaginative and disciplined interpretation, the sole and sufficient norm for theology. Theology is always *beneath* the Scriptures in importance, but Scripture without theology is mute.

The originality and scope of Barth's theology will not be surpassed in this century. Like any original intellectual work, however, it bristles with problems, many of which will be evident as other interpretations of Jesus are considered in the pages which follow. Perhaps the most significant feature for the purposes of this study is Barth's great care that he *not* define what in this book has been called the dimensions of lostness. That reluctance is based on Barth's awareness of how human perception can twist the reality of Christ to fit what in a particular cultural epoch is regarded as the human predicament. In this Barth will always serve as a reminder to subsequent generations of theologians that the *Christ who comes is not the Christ who is expected.* We can never know in advance how the experienced fact of Jesus as Savior will be received. It may be putting too fine a point on it, but the plurality of ways in which Jesus has been understood as Savior in modern theology is in some respects a testimony to Barth's own high respect for the freedom of God to act through God's own Word in Christ in ways which no theology can predict. Indeed, there is a sense in which Barth's own rendering of the Word of God is not a prescriptive or a predictive one. Predictions or prescriptions concerning the work of God's Word are never the prerogative of the theologian.

The Word as Narrative

The theology of Karl Barth, not surprisingly, was both welcomed and rejected wherever his influence was felt. In the United States he found very early supporters following the explosive impact of his commentary on Romans. Indeed, his first professorship was a chair of Reformed Theology at Göttingen founded by American Presbyterians. His German colleagues at Göttingen were not unanimously enthusiastic. Although many have pronounced neoorthodoxy to be in eclipse, the power of Barth's genius and the widespread—thanks largely to him—concern that Christian theology be watchful lest Christianity in America be captured and acculturated and thus lose its critical power are still very much alive. So-called neoorthodox themes are commonly heard in American pulpits and articulated by widely read theologians such as Jürgen Moltmann, Helmut Thielicke, Douglas John Hall, Carl Braaten, and W. Robert Jenson,[17] none of whom is a "Barthian" or a doctrinaire neoorthodox theologian. They and others can usually be counted on to resist all efforts to assimilate the Christian gospel to a cultural fad or fashionable philosophy.

Hans W. Frei cannot, in fairness, be identified as a strict follower of any "school" of theology, but there are in his work affinities to the method which is characteristic of Barth's approach to Christ as the Word. The references in the discussion which follows are all taken from Frei's small volume published in 1975, *The Identity of Jesus Christ: The Hermeneutical Bases of Dogmatic Theology.*[18]

There are two prominent themes in Frei's Christology, "presence" and "narrative"; they are closely related. In simplest terms, one might ask such a question as this, "In light of the historical distance between our time and the life of Jesus, and in view of the pervasive ambiguities in every human effort really to know Jesus, *how can Jesus be present* to us as Savior? Frei's answer is, again in simplest terms, "In the narrative and only in the narrative." Immediately one is curious to know what is meant by "presence" and what is the nature of "narrative" or "story." Frei's small book attempts to address those questions, but it is not difficult to see that when Frei relates the presence of Jesus to narrative it is a version of Barth's identification of Christ with the proclaimed Word. For Barth, theology serves the proclamation of the Word; for Frei theology serves the telling of the narrative. Other similarities are evident. The presence of Jesus is not explainable apart from belief or faith; one must resist, then, trying to explain what presence means or how Jesus is present. Explanations will often slip into psychology or historical memory, neither of which is adequate to convey presence. Neither thinking about Jesus nor reminiscence of Jesus can carry the weight of what Frei speaks of as presence.

Frei's alternative is stated at the outset:

> The governing conviction . . . is that in Jesus Christ identity and presence are so completely one that they are given to us together: We cannot know *who* he is without having him present. But I also want to suggest that if we begin with the often nagging and worrisome questions of *how* Christ is present to us and *how* we can believe in his presence, we shall get nowhere at all. It is far more important and fruitful to ask first, *Who* is Jesus Christ? (p. 4).

Hence the title of Frei's book. Identity precedes presence. To know who Jesus is is already to know Jesus as present. To know him is to have him; it is impossible, once one knows *who* Jesus is, to think of him as absent, so instead of concentrating on the mechanics of presence, faith thinks of the identity of Jesus which—especially in the case of Jesus—is inseparable from presence. Christ's presence is a mystery which cannot be thought; his identity, however, can not only be thought but also known. And when his identity is known, his presence is real as well.

The argument which Frei develops can be stated in two rather simple steps, each of which needs further elaboration:

1. The identity of Jesus can be known.
2. The identity implies the presence.

In short, the presence of Christ—which has become so problematic for contemporary persons who are steeped in historical consciousness—cannot be established by appealing to more and more history. The historical sciences, insists Frei, are only a secondary aid; thus he is unwilling to appeal to any historical descriptions of Jesus, for example, to his alleged historical uniqueness or to his consciousness. History is not the means by which to establish the presence of Jesus Christ, whose earthly career took place so many centuries ago. Frei refuses to employ the methods of historical research. He does not presume to trace the route of Jesus' influence on the church and culture from the past to the present day. Therefore he does not build a foundation out of historical studies and then ask how the personal influence of Jesus can be present for contemporary persons. Instead, Frei begins immediately with the question, Who is Jesus? confident that with the answer to the prior question of Jesus' identity his presence will be real as well.

Nor does Frei tackle the problem of identity (pp. 36ff.) by using psychological or historical categories; instead he uses the category of the self, and in that connection refers both to Kierkegaard ("the self is a relation which relates itself to its own self") and Augustine ("There [i.e., in memory] . . . do I meet with myself, and recall myself—what, when, or where I did a thing, and how I was affected when I did it"). Ultimately, a person's uniqueness, the uniqueness of the self, which is the equivalent of the identity of that person or self, entails two factors. First, the ability of the self to change argues for a certain intentionality which is acted out: intention–action. Second, the self does continue through changes. There is a subject who somehow endures as the one who intends and acts: self-manifestation. Both of these factors together constitute the self. When we ask what gives us access to another self or person, or how we come to know who a person is, the answer can only be the narrative or story of that person's life. Thus, in the special case of Jesus, his identity is rendered for us primarily in the narrative of the New Testament in which there are clues both as to the intention–action of Jesus and the self-manifestation of Jesus. To know the intention–action and the self-manifestation of Jesus is to know his identify and, thus, to have Jesus fully present.

The resurrection narratives are a crucial part of the New Testament. Because none of Frei's project is dependent on historical arguments, he is thus not obliged to defend the historicity of the resurrection of Jesus but to show how, in the resurrection narratives, the identity of Jesus is most clearly rendered. In order to follow his demonstration of how that works, we must keep in mind that identity is understood as both intention–action and subject-manifestation. The intentions of Jesus are acted out; his actions bespeak an intention *and* the subject who intends those actions is manifested in them, even as what (who) is manifested is that subject.

Why is resurrection the key? Because it is not possible to narrate the resurrection accounts and confine our attention to the identity of Jesus alone. After all, what sense does it make to speak of the intention of Jesus in the resurrection when it is not Jesus who raised himself? Thus it is not Jesus alone whose identity is manifested in the resurrection; another subject is required to account for what happens. The narrative of the resurrection is the climax of the story of the crucifixion. Jesus did not crucify himself, although he does intend *some*thing by accepting the actions of those who crucified him; his crucifiers intended something else. In the New Testament telling of it even the actions of those who crucified Jesus are governed by another: God. As the story unfolds there is a decrease of initiative on the part of Jesus. "Nevertheless, Jesus' intentions and actions become increasingly identified with those of the very God who governs the actions of the opponents of Jesus who destroy him." And even though there is a distinction throughout between what God is doing and what Jesus is undergoing ("My God, my God, why hast thou forsaken me?" Mark 15:34), Jesus does not lose his identity. Instead the identity of Jesus and the identity of God are inextricably mixed. In Frei's reading of the crucifixion and resurrection narrative there is a "rising curve or dominance of God's activity over that of Jesus [which] reaches its apex, not in the account of Jesus' death, but in that of his resurrection. . . . It is here—even more than in the crucifixion—that God and God alone is active." Even though the stress is exclusively on God acting—God alone is efficacious in the resurrection narrative—the hand of God "remains completely veiled at this point in the story" (p. 120).

Because God remains hidden (there are few references to God in the resurrection narrative) and because Jesus is nonetheless present as the crucified one now resurrected from the dead, none other than Jesus of Nazareth "marks the presence of the action of God" (p. 121). God is hidden, but Jesus marks the spot where God is active. The identity of Jesus *is* the presence and action of God, and there is no other way than by the narrative to make that point. "The upshot . . . is that the Gospel narrative presents us with neither a simple unification nor a simple distinction between Jesus and God, either in terms of intention–action or of self-manifestation identification. The pattern of their interrelation remains irreducibly complex" (p. 124).

Lest the point about the status of the narrative be missed, Frei repeats a theme familiar to readers of Barth. One could easily interchange *Word* and *narrative* in what follows.

The nature of the narrative therefore imposes a limit on theological comment. It is not likely that we shall be able to go beyond the descriptive accounts presented to us in the Gospels concerning the resurrection and the relation of God's and Jesus' actions. And if we do go beyond them in explanatory endeavors, we are clearly on our own and in speculative territory, just as . . . we are in speculative realms when we look beyond the narrative for the writers' and Jesus' own inner intentions. In that instance, our speculation would be historical . . . But it is never easy and usually not desirable to transform a literary description, such as a narrative sequence, into an *explanatory* scheme using abstract concepts and categories. What is perfectly fitting in a narrative may be banal or absurd in an explanatory scheme drawn from our general experience of occurrences in the world (p. 125).

For the sake of the narrative, Frei admits, theology may have to take the risk of being speculative and to put into abstract and conceptual language what is primarily and most fittingly communicated by narrative. But what is *not* open to theology is to *begin* with conceptual categories and then use the narrative to illustrate or support the conceptual apparatus. Literary form has priority over philosophical categories, and to reverse that sequence is to domesticate the narrative.

Presumably, Professor Frei would be loath to read the New Testament narrative with a soteriological bias, inasmuch as it would distort the narrative in much the same way as preformed conceptual concerns prejudge what the story can possibly mean for us today. If there is a human predicament which inescapably shapes how modern persons will read the narrative, it is precisely the predicament of being historically removed from the events of Jesus' life and death; no theory of history, no psychological or religious program can remove that barrier. To state it somewhat simplistically, for Frei there is no way that the experienced fact of Jesus as Savior can be available to contemporary persons. Until *who* Jesus is (his identity) is a present reality, it is useless to ask how Jesus can be Savior. Obviously, there *is* a predicament which determines to a large extent *how* Frei approaches the New Testament; that is the problem of historical consciousness, which cannot be overcome by piling up more and more historical evidence as the basis for faith in Jesus as the Christ who saves. Because historical evidence is at best relative, it cannot be the foundation for identifying Jesus as the God-man who alone can save.

The Basis of Faith: The Historical Resurrection

Wolfhart Pannenberg dissents from the view that there is no historical evidence upon which to base faith in Jesus. In the mid-1960s the theological world was beginning to take notice of a brilliant new star, the young Wolfhart Pannenberg. It was not until his provocative Christology was translated into English and published as *Jesus—God and Man* in 1968 that the debate about his extraordinary program was taken up in the United States.[19] The similarities as well as the differences between him and Karl Barth are both important and subtle. Of these differences, a major one is Pannenberg's determination to construct theology, and in particular a Christology, "from below" and not "from above," as Barth would have it. It is not so much *what* Pannenberg asserts about Jesus Christ that is so different from Barth's Christology—although there are differences aplenty—but *how* Pannenberg takes up the task.

First, Pannenberg rejects the implicit fideism in Christology from above. It is no longer credible to begin with the merely assumed authority of Scripture as revelation and then on that basis to make assertions about the divinity of Christ. Rather, credibility can be achieved only if one can establish, on the basis of the actual history of Jesus, some evidence which could lead to the conclusion that Jesus is the God-man. The past history of Jesus can be the only foundation of claims for him as the God-man. If there is no *historical* basis, there can be no foundation for faith. Where Pannenberg would agree with Barth is in rejecting all attempts to base Christian theology on contemporary Christian experiences, the favorite strategy of the 19th-century liberals.[20]

Second, Pannenberg notes that Christologies from above rarely pay serious attention to the "distinctive features of the historical man, Jesus of Nazareth." Jesus as the man from Nazareth plays no significant role in Christologies from above. Such Christologies treat Jesus as though he were of secondary importance. These theologies pay significant attention to the man Jesus only when it is Jesus' time to die on the cross.

Third, Christologies from above presume that it is possible to view history from some lofty perspective above history. Pannenberg here joins most 20th-century thinkers in acknowledging that not even theologians can escape "the context of a historically determined human situation."[21] The way anyone thinks, even when thinking theologically, will be relative to the social, historical, and cultural context in which one lives. Christologies from above would be possible only if one could "stand in the position of God himself." Pannenberg does not conclude from this that a "modernist" view of reality should now be the normative perspective for making judgments about Jesus, because, after all, even that view is historically determined and is therefore just as relative as any other. Thus, Pannenberg thinks, Jesus' identity as God incarnate cannot be ruled out in advance on the mere grounds that it is a notion that does not conform to a modern worldview. No human view of things can be taken as final or absolute or somehow immune from historical relativity, regardless of how well established or taken-for-granted it is by the majority of contemporary intellectuals. Pannenberg insists that the question *Who* is Jesus? must be left open to *historical* consideration. This surely contrasts sharply both with Barth's approach (that Scripture be read as faithful testimony to the Word of God as witnessed to by the writers), and with a positivist's view (that Scripture be regarded as the expression of a premodern faith which is no longer tenable for a contemporary person). Pannenberg does not insist that one look at the record from the view of faith, but he does insist that in the name of historical and intellectual honesty a modern person ought to read the record in full recognition that no one's biases should predetermine what can be said about the identity of Jesus.

Who is Jesus? then, is Pannenberg's first question, and in that respect he is in total agreement with Barth and Frei, among others. Christ is *not* known first of all by his benefits. One must first establish that Jesus is the one who *can* deliver salvation before speaking of Jesus as the one who saves. He does agree that "what causes us to ask about the figure of Jesus" is precisely the interest in salvation, but he is at great pains to avoid the "danger that Christology will

be *constructed* out of the soteriological interest." Like Barth, he
will not begin with the *human* question. Even though it may be the
legitimate motive for asking about Christ, it is not a suitable foundation for determining who Christ is. Soteriology is not the basis
for Christology. "The danger becomes acute when [such a] procedure is elevated to a program as by Melanchthon and later Schleiermacher, who constructed his christology by inference from the
experience of salvation."[22] Thus, while Pannenberg will not give a
privileged place to a Christology from above, neither does he look
for the starting place "below" in Christian experience. The only
suitable foundation will be history—specifically the historically verifiable resurrection of Jesus from the dead.

Most historians are likely to reject the contention that the resurrection of Jesus is a verifiable event. Pannenberg argues that such
rejection is itself a questionable judgment for historians to make,
since it goes against the evidence of the New Testament witnesses.
Although there are no reports that anyone actually witnessed Jesus
rising from the tomb, there are numerous reports of those who witnessed the risen Jesus appearing in various situations.[23] For Pannenberg there can be little doubt that biblical scholarship concerning
the resurrection narratives makes it clear that the New Testament,
and especially Paul, intends the material to be "a convincing historical proof by the standards of that time." Admittedly this material
has a special interest in view, but that special interest did not "in-
vent" the proof.[24] Instead, argues Pannenberg, present-day historians are the ones whose modern bias prejudices them against the
witnesses. He concludes that it is at least historically probable that
the witnesses are trustworthy, and that therefore there are historical
reasons for accepting the resurrection. That being the case, the only
"argument" against the testimony of New Testament witnesses
would have to be based on certain prejudices about what is historically possible or impossible. Not even physicists, he writes, would
make such claims for the physical universe because "an individual
event is never completely determined by natural laws. Conformity
to law embraces only one aspect of what happens. From another
perspective, everything that happens is contingent, and the validity
of the laws of nature is itself contingent."[25] If so, there is all the
more reason to be suspicious of the alleged validity of any historical
judgments which declare that the resurrection was impossible. Just

as faith does not make the historicity of an event certain, neither is historical skepticism sufficient reason to dismiss the resurrection as impossible—against the testimony of historical witnesses.[26] Pannenberg's quarrel is not against historical criticism as such. His objection is to those who make claims which go beyond the limitations of historical criticism, namely, either fideistic claims (it happened because faith requires it) or historicistic claims (it could not possibly have happened because laws of history preclude it).

As Pannenberg interprets the New Testament, the resurrection of Jesus, as an actual event of history, is "historically very probable, and that always means in historical inquiry that it is to be presupposed until contrary evidence appears."[27] Only a historian with a "narrow concept of reality" which then dictates that "dead men do not rise" would reject the resurrection of Jesus as historical and go off in search of some other explanation for the Easter story rather than "speak of the resurrection as the explanation that is best established" as the basis of the Easter story.[28]

Pannenberg's essential agreement with Barth now comes into view. The fundamental question for modern theology is the problem of revelation.[29] The Enlightenment and its greatest philosopher, Kant, had destroyed "the old theistic picture of the world" and so one can no longer begin with a concept of God and then ask how that God, so conceived, could be known, or even become flesh. Even if the question of God continues to be asked, in the absence of any credible theistic worldview, there is nothing in modern experience or reason, determined as it is by a nontheistic picture of the world, out of which to fashion an answer to the question.

The "old theistic world picture," in short, has been destroyed. Without that picture functioning as a determining factor in how one thinks or acquires knowledge, knowledge of God becomes very problematic, because the concept of reality on which knowledge is largely based is nontheistic. In other words, knowledge is based on occurrences in history and nature which are themselves preconceived as nontheistic according to the thought-world developed since the Enlightenment. If there is to be any knowledge of God it can only be as God reveals God's own self in a historical occurrence. The historical occurrence of the resurrection is such a self-revelation of God. It also gave to early Christians the impulse to think Christologically "from below," that is, "from Jesus' claim to authority confirmed by the Easter event.'' In spite of the fact that the concepts which were employed foster a way of *thinking* that moves from above to below (e.g., the Son of man Christology), the historical impetus for that thought came from below, namely, the resurrection of Jesus from the dead.

Apocalypse: Toward a Theory of History

It is a familiar axiom today that all facts, whether historical or scientific, are theory-dependent. Even skepticism about the historicity of the resurrection of Jesus from the dead is dependent on a certain theory of history, or more properly on a certain horizon of expectation. One's *outlook on* history will significantly influence what one *looks out for.* What one actually will notice as historical will be largely determined by one's outlook on history. Witnesses to the resurrection of Jesus could take note of that event and report it as historical because their outlook on history was an apocalyptic one which was not biased against dead men rising. They were able actually to witness what had happened.

The apocalyptic conceptual world is, one might say, the "theory" of history upon which the "fact" of resurrection depends. Whether or not modern persons can accept apocalyptic as a binding theory for their own reading of history, it is absolutely essential, in Pannenberg's view, for understanding claims made for Christ. It is not a disposable matter; it may be premodern and even prescientific, but its truthfulness is crucial for Christology. "One must be clear about the fact that when one discusses the truth of the apocalyptic expectation of a future judgment and a resurrection from the dead, one is dealing directly with the basis of the Christian faith" so that "apart from that horizon of the apocalyptic expectation," all claims about Jesus as the ultimate revelation of God are "incomprehensible."[30] Not only does the fact (resurrection) lose its credibility as fact but the meaning of the fact is lost as well.

In simplest terms, the apocalyptic conceptual world (on which the recognition of the historicity of the resurrection depends) holds that the meaning or essence of history and humanity lies in the future. The meaning or truth of any person's life, of any epoch of history, or of any culture cannot be discerned by tracing out the complex web of causal connections from the past to the present. Neither can it be discerned by trying to uncover philosophically the underlying essential reality of which each life or epoch is a partial manifestation. "The essence of man is not to be sought in what is already realized in man, but it still comes to him from his future. The essence of man is the destiny that still lies beyond the empirical content of man's present."[31] Pannenberg draws on biblical scholarship to support his contention that the conceptual world of Scripture is apocalyptic. "Apocalyptic is the mother of theology" became the rallying cry of the Pannenberg circle. But what appeal does an apocalyptic view hold for people today?

One answer is that it provides a framework for understanding the Bible (or at least some of it; not every book in the Bible is suffused with apocalyptic, e.g., the wisdom literature, the Gospel of John, and Luke-Acts). It is also a strategy for carrying on a discussion with modern historians, some of whom may indeed be unaware of how their historicism has led them to make unwarranted judgments about the historical foundations of Christianity.

Lostness as Hopelessness: Jesus as the End

Apocalyptic Christology as Pannenberg develops it may have an even more basic appeal when one notices how he draws together revelation and salvation. At bottom, Pannenberg relates salvation to human hopes and longings. The essence of human beings is their destiny, according to Pannenberg, and thus if humans are cut off from their destiny, they are cut off from what they essentially are. Not to know one's destiny is to be hopeless and lost, that is, deprived of essential humanity. To know the End for which we are destined is to be saved from the lostness of hopelessness and thus to be able to live. As an illustration of what this means in practice, Pannenberg cites, among other things, modern medicine, which "has recognized that radical hopelessness has death as its consequence."[32] Revealed knowledge of the End, therefore, is also salvation, because it satisfies everyone's quest for personal destiny. Revelation and salvation are inseparable and are dependent on an apocalyptic view of history and reality. In other words, if one *knows* that one's destiny has been fulfilled by an historical event in which the End has already been revealed, then one is saved from hopelessness. The future in which one's destiny and essence lie is no longer uncertain. But as long as the destiny of humankind is unknown or as long as there is no historical basis for believing that it has been or will be fulfilled, then there is no hope. This is so because hope—an essential fact of humanity—can be meaningful only if it has a basis in history. This is especially apparent in regard to one's own death. "The phenomenology of hope indicates that it belongs to the essence of conscious human existence to hope beyond death." [33]

Thus, although Pannenberg, like Barth, will not permit soteriology to determine Christology—lest some subjective human need be projected on the objective reality of Christ—there is nonetheless in Pannenberg's work a dominant perception of the human predicament for which Christ is the Savior. His entire Christological masterwork is a correlation of (1) Christ as the End of history already revealed in the resurrection and (2) the human quest for a basis for hope. Pannenberg assumes that a person's essential nature is completely determined "not by what is already realized" or achieved through genetic endowment and previous efforts, but "that it still comes to him from his future" (see note 31). He assumes also that this essence or destiny is revealed through Jesus. None of this, of course, is comprehensible unless one adopts an apocalyptic view which alone can ground Christology "from below."

According to Karl Barth, the worldview which Western civilization had developed since the Enlightenment had virtually imprisoned Christian thinkers, whose acculturated theology could not allow the Bible to speak on its own terms. Proclamation of Christ as the Word of God was filtered through the theologians' perception of reality, and was thus so thinned out that it gave no offense to the presumed canons of intelligibility. Theology's role, he thundered, is not to sit in judgment over the Word, but to respond to that Word with proclamation fit for the times. He was no literalist, nor was he a romantic about some previous age. He was no "modernist" either, since he seriously doubted the capacity of either religious sensibility or philosophical perspicacity to grasp the truth to which the Scriptures witness. He went beyond modern religiosity, modern empiricism, and modern positivism and thus may have anticipated some features of the postmodern hermeneutic of suspicion.

Pannenberg raises the ante on Barth's proposal. He shares Barth's suspicion of reductionist approaches to the biblical witness. Historical critics of the Bible have often simply adopted the modern prejudice against the premodern—i.e., apocalyptic—view of the biblical witnesses. Their prejudice leads them to say that the resurrection is impossible. They fail to be suspicious of their own prejudice, and thus, in a most unhistorical way, dismiss witnesses whose testimony can only be challenged by countertestimony and not by the philosophical prejudice of the historian.

Barth merely *assumes* that the scriptural witness to Jesus Christ is the revealed Word, thus bypassing all the questions a modern historian might raise. Pannenberg, by contrast, challenges historians of the Bible to be more historical and to recognize that the resurrection of Jesus from the dead is not only plausible but, given the underlying apocalyptic view of history, is God's revelation of the End and, as such, is the salvation of humankind from hopelessness. What is at stake here is the knowledge of God which is simultaneously the salvation of humanity.

Just as Karl Barth could say that Christology should be judged by whether it helps to bring a person to the experience of the disciples on the Mount of Transfiguration, so Pannenberg can write that the saving character that belongs to Jesus is determined by whether Jesus is understood as "the *fulfillment* of the hopes and deep longing of humanity. There is no salvation that is not related to the needs of those to whom it is imparted."[34] Both Barth and Pannenberg warn against constructing a Christology on the basis of subjective perceptions of the human condition; yet both agree that ultimately a Christology is to be judged by whether it can credibly render Jesus as Savior. Such credibility of Jesus as Savior is dependent on a shared view of lostness either as unbelief (Barth) or hopelessness (Pannenberg).

Chapter Three

THE SAVIOR
AS NEW BEING AND AS
CREATIVE
TRANSFORMATION

Paul Tillich was no less concerned than Karl Barth *that* theology serve the proclamation of Jesus as the Christ. Tillich and Barth were both born in 1886 and participated in the same intellectual and cultural crises of modern Western civilization. Throughout their careers they were in nearly total disagreement about *how* theology should serve proclamation. Tillich compared Barth's kerygmatic theology to throwing a stone at the human situation without bothering to discover what common ground the Christian message of salvation might already share with existence in general.[1] Tillich, unlike Barth, was confident that salvation was not a totally alien notion and that apologetic theology could demonstrate that point with an adequate conceptual system.

The christological problem started . . . when men became aware of their existential predicament and asked whether their predicament could be overcome through a new state of reality. In an anticipatory way the christological problem appeared in the prophetic and apocalyptic expectation. The foundations for a formulated christology were provided by the way the writers of the New Testament applied symbols to Jesus, whom they called "the Christ.". . . . The early church began to interpret the christological symbols in conceptual terms available through the work of Greek philosophy. . . . Whether or not these concepts were adequate to the interpretation of the Christian message remains a permanent question for theology. But it is wrong to reject a priori the use of Greek concepts by the early church. There was no alternative.[2]

With that historical comment Paul Tillich underscores a basic theme of this book, namely, that formulating a *theory* about Christ is necessary in order to carry forward the experienced fact of Jesus as Savior, and that there is no alternative to using the best conceptual tools available. Tillich argued that a Christology—though a theoretical construction—must always be tested against the experienced fact of salvation. He summarized this point in these words:

The early church was well aware that christology is an existentially necessary, though not a theoretically interesting, work of the church. Its ultimate criterion, therefore, is existential itself. It is "soteriological," i.e., *determined* by the question of salvation.[3]

Whereas Barth and Pannenberg agreed that a soteriological question can be the *motive* behind all Christological formulations, it is clear that they want to minimize, if not to eliminate, the influence the existential question can have on the definition of Christ. They quite deliberately constructed Christologies which, as far as possible, transcend subjective perception of what Christ ought to be. Tillich, on the other hand, is very forthright. "Christology is a function of soteriology. The problem of soteriology creates the christological question and gives direction to the christological answer. This criterion has been presupposed in all christological assertions."[4]

For Tillich, then, the soteriological problem is the criterion by which to measure all Christologies: Do they preserve everything implied by the church's faith in Jesus as the Christ, that is, as the one who saves? A fair and balanced test of any Christology, including Tillich's, is whether the Christ who is presented can be identified and received as Savior. Savior from what? "From the old being, that is, from existential estrangement and its self-destructive

consequences."⁵ Tillich does not believe that his program is unique,
but that soteriological issues were presupposed in all Christological
assertions and that faith in Jesus as Savior obliges anyone holding
that faith to "ask in what sense and in what way Jesus as the Christ
is the Savior or, more precisely, in what way the unique event of
Jesus as the Christ has universal significance for every human being
and, indirectly, for the universe as well."⁶

Jesus as Savior implies a predicament. The predicament, from
which Jesus saves, will always provide the terms required for defining who Christ is. The terms are required for the theoretical task
of defining Christ, but theology should never become so totally
dependent on any terms or concepts that it loses its own freedom.

What is at stake in all this is that in order for Jesus as Savior to
be experienced, theology must be free to use whatever conceptual
tools are reasonably adequate for communicating the message of
Jesus as Savior. The conceptual apparatus of theology, then, has a
status and function similar to that of myths and symbols in expressing
and defining the claims made by the Christian community. Tillich
insisted that myths and symbols "must be criticized on the basis of
their power to express what they are supposed to express, namely,
in this instance, the New Being in Jesus as the Christ."⁷ In Tillich's
system, that means nothing less than the experienced fact of Jesus
as Savior.

Tillich draws the conceptual language with which to construct his
Christology from the philosophy of being. In order for his own
Christology to meet the soteriological test, Tillich must go back and
lay a new apologetic foundation for theology. He must show how
a philosophy of being can give a persuasive explication of the human
predicament from which Christ, whom Tillich accordingly reinter-
prets as the New Being, is the Savior.⁸ Tillich, unlike Karl Barth,
believed that a partnership between philosophy and theology was
possible and necessary for the task of constructing a suitable Christology. He did not think that when theology adapts the Christian
message to a philosophy appropriate to "the modern mind" it thereby surrenders what is essential and unique to the Christian tradition.
Indeed he insisted that without such an apologetic theology "traditional Christianity would have become narrow and superstitious"
and the general culture would have been deprived of what it needs

from Christianity.[9] For Tillich the relationship between the Christian tradition and the general human situation is irreducibly ambiguous and cannot be described merely in terms of sharp contrasts.

During World War I Pastor Karl Barth was preparing his commentary on Romans, the bombshell which exploded all pretensions of merging the Word of God with the aspirations of high German culture. Tillich was serving in the Kaiser's army. He had entered the military chaplaincy as a German patriot and saw many friends killed in the trenches. The threat of nonbeing was a daily fact for him during that time. After the war, Tillich, like Barth, taught in Germany. In the early thirties, when his protests against the Nazis cost him a prestigious professorship, he came to the United States where, as an immigrant, he joined the company of German intellectuals who had taken up teaching positions in America. For Barth, expulsion from Germany meant returning to Switzerland, his homeland, but for Tillich it meant leaving his homeland, learning a new language, and trying to make his complex theology understood in a significantly different cultural situation. As he was to remark many times, he lived and thought "on the boundary," where a Christian thinker's only alternative is to be an apologetic theologian.

Lostness as Estrangement

Tillich commonly used the term *estrangement* to speak of lostness, but it is a term which he never restricted to an individualistic interpretation, and certainly not to merely psychological dimensions of human existence. It infects not only human beings but their world. It is a term borrowed from existentialist philosophy.

> Existentialism has analyzed the "old eon," namely, the predicament of man and his world in the state of estrangement. In doing so, existentialism is a natural ally of Christianity. Immanuel Kant once said that mathematics is the good luck of human reason. In the same way one could say that existentialism is the good luck of Christian theology.[10]

Existentialism is the philosophy which, in the 20th century, best conveys the tragic break or gap between the world as it actually exists and Scripture's depiction of creation before the Fall. Tillich rejected earlier "essentialist" philosophies, for example, Hegel's "classical essentialist" philosophy in which "the world is the self-realization of the divine mind . . . [and] existence is the expression of essence and not the fall away from it."[11] In contrast to Hegel's notion that the "Fall is not a break, but an imperfect fulfillment,"[12] Tillich believed the Fall to be far more radical than that. *Estrangement* is the most apt term for describing the deep and tragic consequences of the Fall as the disrelation between God and the world.

Indeed, Tillich has driven estrangement so deeply into the structure of existence and has thrown it so broadly into the far reaches of the universe that some have criticized him for "ontologizing" sin and thereby minimizing the concrete historical character of sin. The "ontological overpowers the historical," is Reinhold Niebuhr's well-known complaint.[13] But Tillich was concerned that estrangement not be trivialized. Therefore he did not make an absolute distinction between estrangement as it infects human beings in history and as it infects the rest of creation. "Christianity knows and can never give up its knowledge of the tragic universality of existential estrangement" and therefore must "reject the idealistic separation of an innocent nature from guilty man." Human beings are part of the universe. It "works through us." Humans and the universe participate in each other inseparably.[14] The world, because it, too, is fallen, prevents human beings from returning to some presumably innocent nature for release from estrangement. No one can escape. No one can find salvation from the ills of human society through a romantic return to an imaginary uncontaminated natural order. All of creation, although it is "good in its essential character," as soon as it is actualized falls into universal estrangement.[15]

It should be clear that estrangement, in the thought of Tillich, is a universal *condition*. It catches all humans in the same predicament of the lostness of alienation. Humanity shares that predicament with the universe in general, that is, *all* creatures are alienated from the power of being. On the other hand, humans are distinct from the rest of creation because, in humans, estrangement is sin. In humans estrangement has a different character, because it includes the personal decision to "turn away from that to which one belongs."[16] In humans, then, estrangement is both a tragic condition and an accusation. All share responsibility for sin. The crucial point to note here is that *Tillich does not confine his description of the human predicament to the God-self polarity;* thus the structure of estrangement, whose peculiar character in humans must be called sin, is a universal structure found in all existence. This means, then, that animals and atoms are caught in the condition of universal estrangement together with humans but, unlike humans, animals and atoms do not sin.

Many have called Tillich an existentialist theologian, but this is only partially correct. Tillich's use of existentialism is a tactical device by which he is able to uncover the universal—which is to say, ontological—scope of estrangement by using the human self as the primary specimen within existence. Every self is part of the universe. What is characteristic of a part will be true of the whole. Existentialist philosophy is especially accurate in its analysis of the *human* predicament for which Christ is the answer. In order for theology to speak of the "tragic universality of existential estrangement" it needs more than existentialist philosophy's focus on the self as it relates to itself or even—as some existentialists might put it—as the self relates to God. If theology is to clarify the *universality* of estrangement, it must use a philosophy which deals with universal structures, namely, a philosophy of being. Thus a philosophy of being extends the estrangement, known *immediately* by the self in its self-knowledge, to include the *indirect* knowledge of the estrangement of all existence. Tillich focuses on the human self as the primary point of entry into universal structures of being; selves have access to those structures from the "inside," so to speak.

Tillich's view of the world—of existence in general—is utterly bleak. Estrangement profoundly threatens being. Unless there is salvation of the world—i.e., of being—salvation of *human* selves will only be partial. Tillich will not limit salvation to humans snatched out of the world and safely set apart from the structures of being. Nonbeing threatens to suck all that exists into nothingness, and therefore salvation of humanity apart from salvation of the world—of being itself—is inconceivable. It is not sufficient to speak of Jesus as the one who primarily reconciles the God-self disrelation. The whole of existence is estranged from God. The God-world relation, too, is in tragic disrepair, and therefore it is absolutely critical that theology somehow address the lostness that threatens the world lest salvation be limited in its scope to the peculiar existential distress of human beings. A philosophy of being is supremely critical for that theological task. But one can only "get at" the structures of being by investigating them from "inside" the self. Because the self is correlated to the world by virtue of its participation in the ontological structures common to *both* self and world, the whole universe in its estrangement can be thus indirectly known.[17]

Most of the biblical writers merely *assumed* that the world is upheld by God in God's ultimate and universal power of being. From that assumption they could then go on to describe God's revelation of God's will in historical events. Tillich thinks that contemporary, intellectually honest persons cannot easily assume—as did the biblical writers—that God is the ultimate basis of all history and creation. What Scripture merely *assumes,* a contemporary person must *argue* for in terms of a contemporary and appropriate philosophical description of the structures of reality.[18] Tillich develops this description in volume 1 of the *Systematic Theology,* Part II, "Being and God." Throughout this extended philosophical description he seems to have had his eye all the while on Christ, the *New* Being. It was necessary that the *terms* for that subsequent *Christological* formulation be laid out by speaking of the God-world polarity. The God-world relation has to do with the question of being itself, whose structures can be known independently of Jesus. But if Jesus is eventually to be *thought* of and re-presented as Savior of the structures of being (the God-world *dis*relation) then—lest Christology fail the soteriological test—the structures of reality must be investigated and set forth.

It is in the interest of showing how the significance of Jesus Christ, the New Being, is *universal* that Tillich is willing to engage in the unavoidable risk of proposing an ontology in the first volume of the *Systematic Theology.* Tillich, therefore, makes himself extremely vulnerable to the accusation that he was not building his system on Scripture but on philosophy. Such charges are simply not fair to his intention. Because the biblical assumptions about God and the world are no longer believable to the contemporary thinker, theology must offer concepts that *are* intelligible. Without them, the Christian message of Jesus Christ as Savior cannot be communicated. Tillich's *intention,* one might say, *is* biblical, but he obviously does not try to preserve outmoded features of the biblical worldview, which are no longer tenable. He offers what he thinks is a worldview that is not only compatible with the biblical message but also intelligible to contemporary persons. His program is similar to Bultmann's attempts to liberate faith from a premodern view of reality, but dissimilar insofar as Tillich goes on to offer what he regards as a modern, workable view of reality. If Christians want to communicate the truth of Scripture, they have no alternative.

Tillich's ontology, which he places in the service of communicating the Christian message, cannot be sketched here. Many have rejected his scheme as not adequate for what he intends, namely, an intelligible replacement for the prescientific ontology assumed by the scriptural writers. Many readers, including philosophers, are either baffled by Tillich or simply amazed that anyone would dare attempt something as anachronistic as a philosophy of being which, after all, may be no more acceptable to moderns than the prescientific views found in Scripture. But no one can help but be impressed with the elegant and imaginative structure into which are woven the ontological elements of the philosophy of being. When Tillich eventually turns to his Christology and there employs that conceptuality, he is in a position to describe the consequences of ontological estrangement within the actual lived existence of human beings. The payoff, one might say, is one of the most compelling descriptions of the pervasiveness and destructiveness of sin ever written. The marks of human estrangement stalking every aspect of life are exposed in gripping, even frightening, detail. All human beings are ensnared in consequences of their own guilt. The world—the structure of existence whose entire being is tied up with the human being—*that* world shakes to its very foundation. Nonbeing threatens not only humanity but even the structures of being upon which every human depends. And there is no way by which human beings can rescue themselves from the perilousness and threat of existence. By means of his ontology Tillich exposes the futility of all ways of self-salvation. Neither religion, social custom, legalistic rigor, ascetic flight, nor cultic, sacramental, and devotional exercises can save humanity.[19]

A strict empiricist would surely wonder how Tillich can know so much. His claims about the dangerous flaws, the threatening cracks and the unstable structures of being are nothing short of universal. Unlike Barth, he does not base such claims exclusively on the revelation of the Word. The universal condition of estrangement from the Power which upholds being can be simply uncovered by examining oneself (the existentialist move) and then extending outwardly what is learned *there* by way of a philosophy of being. Because human beings are bound up with all being, with all that is actual, with all that has being (the ontological move), no one can easily escape the conclusion—short of numbing one's consciousness and shutting down all awareness of oneself and of the self's connection with the world—that the threat of nonbeing which haunts the estranged self also threatens the world in its estrangement.

One must note, finally, that although Tillich's description of lostness is relatively independent of the biblical revelation, it is not built upon a superficial and subjective assessment of human desire. Lostness as alienation or estrangement is a universal condition confronting all humanity—indeed all creatures. Humans are profoundly threatened and cannot save themselves because, at bottom, the threat is universal. The world itself would be utterly doomed if the Power of Being, God (Tillich's term is Being Itself or the Ground of Being), were withdrawn. The threat of lostness is an objective condition which no one can escape; it is not merely a subjectively based opinion which can be avoided or altered.

Even though Tillich's argument for lostness is indebted as much to an existential analysis of the self as to an exegetical analysis of Scripture, the objectivity of lostness is not compromised thereby.[20] Scripture points to the universal character of lostness, as in the account of the Fall, or the many instances of self-destructive sin condemned in the prophetic writings. But for Tillich the work of poets, artists, novelists, and playwrights is no less vivid in disclosing the deep underlying fault weakening every foundation which humans try to lay as the basis for constructing their lives.[21]

Jesus as the New Being

Who Jesus *is* as the Christ—in the *thought* of any theologian—is determined by *what* Jesus must be able to *do* in order to save humanity from the predicament which threatens. What Jesus can do, in turn, implies something about *who* Jesus must be that he has the power and authority to carry it out. His person and work are inseparable in actuality, even if in *thinking* about Jesus we are obliged to make the distinction.[22] To cite Tillich again, "The problem of soteriology creates the christological question and gives direction to the christological answer. . . . This criterion has been presupposed in all christological assertions. . . ."[23] And so, as in the case of Barth, even if the human predicament is perceived as the total inability of human beings to know the depths of the predicament in which they are trapped, or the adamant refusal to admit such, then *that* condition of lostness (abysmal unbelief) determines who Christ is construed to be, namely, the Word which breaks through and can alone reveal the truth of lostness as well as salvation from unbelief. In Barth's case *revelation* as the Word is what Jesus must *be* in order to do what must be done, namely, to save humanity from the predicament of unbelief. In Tillich's own case, the New Being is what Jesus must be in order to save from the predicament of estrangement.

One must remember that Tillich goes to great pains to preserve the paradoxical character of Christological thinking. The pervasiveness of estrangement is simply part of existence confronting and engulfing all of us. The predicament of estrangement itself prompts all kinds of strategies by which we would try to save ourselves. Estrangement does threaten, it does generate varieties of expectations of what might save, and it does stimulate thinkers to propose all sorts of interpretations of the human situation. But Jesus as the New Being is not merely an abstract idea which Tillich bounces off the hard reality of estranged existence. The New Being is more than a logical idea derived from the facts of existence. Rather, the appearance of the New Being contradicts ordinary logical expectations; it is a paradox.

Tillich believes that his ontological description of estrangement is severely limited to just that: a description of estrangement. It cannot generate a saving event. At best, ontology can offer a theory, but a theory is not yet a fact or an event. At worst, Tillich's own vision of the tragic universality of estrangement can lead to despair. There is no escape, no self-salvation of being, because all creatures (beings) are confined to the limits of existence and any being thus strictly confined is itself estranged and therefore cannot be a candidate for Savior. And so, if there *were* to appear under the conditions of existence One who could save, such a One would be a paradox in "the literal sense of the word." Tillich is precise in what he means by paradox: "That is paradoxical which contradicts the *doxa,* the opinion which is based on the whole of ordinary human experience, including the empirical and the rational."[24] Jesus as New Being is paradoxical in the strict sense that the phrase "contradicts the opinion (*doxa*) derived from man's existential predicament and all expectations imaginable on the basis of this predicament. . . . It is an offense against man's unshaken reliance upon himself, his self-saving attempts and his resignation to despair. Against each of these three attitudes the manifestation of the New Being in Christ is judgment and promise."[25] Thus the assertion that this man, Jesus, is the New Being is paradoxical because it goes against "man's self-understanding and expectations" which have been inescapably shaped by the all-embracing condition of estrangement. New Being is a paradox, then, in the sense that it is "a new reality, not a logical riddle," a reality which defies ordinary—which is to say, estranged—modes of understanding.

Human beings are doomed to the self-destructive conditions of estrangement. Only a saving event in real history can rescue them. "If there were no personal life in which existential estrangement had been overcome, the New Being would have remained a quest and an expectation and would not be a reality in time and space."[26] Jesus, for Tillich, is the counterevidence which implies that estrangement is *not* the final word, that salvation *is* possible in a world like this. In Jesus the "tragic universality of existential estrangement" is overcome.

Just as humans can have access to the universal dimensions of lostness only by first investigating the person-as-self and then moving outward to the structures of being with an appropriate philosophical system, they can likewise only have access to the New Being overcoming lostness-as-estrangement if the New Being actually happens in a personal life. Whatever "happens to man happens to all realms of life, for in man all levels of being are present. . . . For this reason the philosophers of the Renaissance called man the 'microcosmos.' " Tillich accepts the interconnectedness of the human with the universe because it "gives cosmic significance to the person and confirms the insight that only in a personal life can the

New Being manifest itself.''[27] Tillich's procedure, then, is to show how, in the personal life of Jesus, estrangement is overcome. If it happens *there* it must be a reality at work throughout the universe— given the ontological principle by which whatever happens in *any* entity happens universally by universal participation. The good news is that it *has* happened in Jesus: in this one personal life, estrangement has been overcome. No one should be doomed to the lostness of estrangement any longer. "To experience the New Being in Jesus as the Christ means to experience the power in him which has conquered existential estrangement in himself and in everyone who participates in him."[28]

Tillich points out that Jesus was clearly a historical person who participated in and was tempted by everything that assails all persons caught in the snares of estrangement. Jesus experienced (1) the temptation of unbelief, which is to regard oneself, instead of God, as the center; (2) the temptation of hubris, which is to regard oneself, instead of God, as the highest; and (3) the temptation of concupiscence, which is to regard oneself, instead of God, as unlimited and universal.[29] Jesus was completely human, historical, and finite and therefore was sorely tempted by these "marks of estrangement"; but, as Tillich reads the New Testament, "there are, in spite of all tensions, no traces of estrangement between [Jesus] and God and consequently between him and himself and between him and his world" (Tillich here means the world as it essentially is, not as it is in its fallen state). The absence of estrangement in Jesus, therefore, means that Jesus, in spite of genuine temptation, does not succumb to unbelief, hubris, or concupiscence.[30] "There are no traces" of the marks of estrangement in Jesus. The absence of such can only be accounted for by *the unbroken unity between Jesus and God.*[31]

> This is the picture of the New Being in Jesus as the Christ. It is not the picture of a divine-human automaton without serious temptation, real struggle, or tragic involvement in the ambiguities of life. Instead of that, it is the picture of a personal life which is subjected to all the consequences of existential estrangement but wherein estrangement is conquered in himself and a permanent unity is kept with God. Into this unity he accepts the negativities of existence without removing them . . . [but] by transcending them in the power of this unity.[32]

Although for Tillich soteriology guides every Christological proposal, the terms *Savior* and *salvation* are not discussed explicitly until the last few pages in the second volume of *Systematic Theology*. At that point Tillich introduces the distinction between salvation in the ultimate sense and salvation as it is variously understood. Tillich has mostly avoided the terms *Savior* and *salvation*. For him, Jesus Christ as the New Being who overcomes the tragic universality of estrangement is a reality so profound, fundamental, central, and all-embracing that it must not be prematurely confused with the many local understandings of salvation which have been popular in the history of the churches. Such understandings confine "salvation" or "Jesus as Savior" to ecclesiastical definitions. These are, he thinks, "limited" meanings. He clearly wants to include them as specific meanings, but all of them fail to grasp the *universal* import of Christ as the New Being. Therefore, none of the following partial understandings of salvation can be regarded as the fundamental meaning.

> For the early Greek church death and error were the things from which one needed and wanted to be saved. In the Roman Catholic church salvation is from guilt and its consequences in this and the next life (in purgatory and hell). In classical Protestantism salvation is from the law, its anxiety-producing and its condemning power. In pietism and revivalism salvation is the conquest of the godless state through conversion and transformation for those who are converted. In ascetic and liberal Protestantism salvation is the conquest of special sins and progress toward moral perfection.[33]

In this passage Tillich obviously shares a concern similar to Barth's and Pannenberg's—that Christology not be built on the too narrow base of what is "needed and wanted" within any particular tradition of Christianity. Instead, his program is to derive Christology, and thus a broader understanding of salvation, "from the appearance of Jesus as the Christ," and in that way to define salvation more broadly and more inclusively. He does not reject the narrower views of salvation listed above, but includes them in the broader view. Tillich thinks salvation can be linked in the modern era with its "original meaning of salvation (from *salvus,* 'healed')," so that, for our time, "healing" might be the most adequate interpretation of salvation. Furthermore, salvation as healing "corresponds to the state of estrangement characteristic of existence. In this sense, healing means reuniting that which is estranged, giving a center to what is split, overcoming the split between God and man, man and his world, man and himself. Out of this interpretation of salvation, the concept of the New Being has grown . . ." and can include the previous, but limited, understandings as well as the understanding of salvation as the fulfillment of the "ultimate meaning of one's existence. . . ."[34]

A further advantage of interpreting salvation in terms of healing is that salvation derived from Jesus as the New Being can then be integrated with the "processes of salvation, i.e., healing, which occur throughout all history." Tillich rejects the "absolute alternative between salvation and condemnation" which insists that one is not saved unless there is an explicit encounter with Jesus as the Christ. Instead, he writes, "Only if salvation is understood as healing and saving power through the New Being in all history is the problem put on another level. *In some degree, all men participate in the healing power of the New Being.* Otherwise, they would have no being. The self-destructive consequences of estrangement would have destroyed them."[35] In actual existence no one is totally healed, not even those who have encountered Jesus as the New Being. Even so, just *to be* is evidence of the presence of healing power to some *degree*. But the partial, unfinished character of healing "drives us to the eschatological." In historical existence there can be no final salvation.

Tillich reserves the *ultimate* sense of the term *salvation* for the New Being which appeared historically in Jesus as the Christ, overcoming estrangement. But if there is no final salvation in history, what can it mean that ultimate salvation has appeared? How is salvation in the ultimate sense disclosed in Jesus the Christ? For Tillich, the ultimacy of Jesus as the Christ is that "he is the ultimate *criterion* of every healing and saving process" (emphasis added). On the other hand, where there is healing, i.e., salvation, those who are healed remain in "a state of relativity with respect to salvation." What is *final* or ultimate *within* history is not total and unambiguous salvation, but rather that there is now available a final *criterion* or norm—Jesus as the Christ who is the New Being—by which every instance of healing or saving must be judged.[36] What is ultimate about Jesus is that in him the ultimate criterion has taken the form of the New Being.[37]

Ultimacy: Being or Becoming?

In Tillich's view there had to be some bridge between historic Christianity and the culture in which Christians live, and so he proposed some mediating concepts by which faith could be communicated. Those concepts cannot be derived exclusively from Christian faith, or else theology would illumine nothing except itself and would be utterly isolated from common experience and thought, which in Tillich's view is precisely the pitfall into which Barth fell by refusing to coordinate faith in Christ with other areas of knowledge. Barth, on the one hand, rejected what had historically been a goal of theology: a total view of reality in which all claims for knowledge can be honored and have at least partial autonomy. Tillich, on the other hand, accepted that broader understanding of theology. Through a philosophy of being he sought to demonstrate how to correlate Christian faith with reason, the common structures of existence, universal history, and culture in general. His tool for doing that was a philosophy of being or a general description of ultimate reality. For Tillich ultimacy is best described in terms of being, and the Ultimate of ultimate reality—God—is Being Itself or the Ground of Being.

Tillich's theology, and hence his Christology, is an illustration of Barth's warning against linking theology too closely to philosophy. Philosophical fashions change.

> Philosophy, rightly or wrongly, has learned to do without the idea of "Being." The dominant modern vision of reality does not seem to allow a place for such a concept, or at least it renders such a concept problematical. Hence, the fundamental principle of Tillich's theology is not anchored in universal reason as he hopes, but in a particular vision of reality which is no longer dominant.[38]

Thus John Cobb, perhaps the most influential and creative thinker among the so-called process theologians, has exposed the weakness of Tillich's philosophical theology: its linkage with a philosophical view of reality makes it no more reliable as a bridge to the culture than the readiness of the culture's philosophers to agree with the view of reality presupposed and argued for in Tillich's theology. In short, Tillich's theology is dependent for its apologetic power on the persuasiveness of philosophical arguments for "being" as the ultimate feature of reality. Nevertheless, John Cobb agrees totally with Tillich's apologetic intention to establish a bridge between Christianity and secular culture while totally rejecting Barth's program of constructing theology on foundations that are utterly independent of philosophy. It is not a question *whether* theology should or should not employ philosophy, but *which* philosophy to use and *how* to use it.[39] For process theologians such as John Cobb the philosophy of choice is the philosophy of *becoming* rather than philosophies of being or of substance.

With Barth's warning against reliance on philosophy in mind, one might well ask, "Why take the chance?" The fact that most theologians, beginning with the earliest Christian thinkers, have done so is not sufficient reason. Cobb argues that what is at stake is Christianity's distinctive and fundamental "vision of reality" upon which all its beliefs depend. This "vision of reality"—implied by the Scriptures—is in danger of being suppressed, or replaced, by a competing nontheistic vision of reality. If this alternative view were accepted as authoritative, Christian theology would be impossible, because theology's claims would then be contrary to the authoritative view of reality. Process theologians like Cobb argue for a philosophy of becoming which will be a bridge between the biblical view of reality and the view of reality which is implied by the physical, social, and psychological sciences.

One might pursue the bridge metaphor further. No bridge can be constructed until a foundation is established on both shores. Such construction on both sides also means a degree of destruction: dynamiting and digging beneath the surface in order to reach a depth sufficient to bear the foundations for the bridge. One cannot assume that the mere surface (let us say) either of biblical faith or of scientific/technological reason will reveal the truth embedded within it. Each "side" has been often superficially interpreted, and those surperficialities must be destroyed—that is, criticized—by an adequate philosophical instrument in order to uncover the deeper layer of reality which can bear the foundations for the bridge. At this point the bridge metaphor must be abandoned, because it hints at rocklike foundations when in fact—in reality—the underlying character of reality is not rocklike at all. Reality instead has the character—regardless of how deeply one digs—of motion, event, flow, energy, change, and, thus, process. Hence the bridge metaphor must give way to the metaphor of conversation or interaction among various ways of thinking, or among various points of view. All speakers in a conversation are equally caught up in the world-in-process. Interaction is not between fixed positions but it is conversation and communication among living, thinking, acting persons who are at the same time being swept along within the flow of historical and natural change.

It is misleading to think that process theologians try to build a bridge anchored in unmovable rock on both sides. Cobb and others like him take it as a given that whether one is a physicist, linguist, psychologist, anthropologist, historian, or theologian, there is no unmovable or unmoving Ground over which the stream flows, and that there are no fixed boundaries between which reality as process moves and by means of which one can take the measure of its direction or velocity. All modes of thinking, including theological thinking, are carried on by thinkers whose very *thoughts* are themselves relative events—all the while being swept along within the oceanic current of events constituting reality in process. There is no fixed place to stand, no place to *be*. "Ultimate reality" cannot be characterized as "being" which is somehow anchored—however precariously—in the Ground of Being. All positions—including theological ones—are relativized by the inescapable flow in which thinkers, speakers, actors, and all entities without exception are carried forward, whether aware of it or not. Ultimacy is *becoming* rather than *being*. Even God—however qualitatively different God may be—is not exempt from living within the flow of reality.

Although all positions are relative, Cobb argues, Christian theology does have a distinctive commitment to a certain way of seeing, valuing, or interpreting reality-as-process. Christian faith cannot credibly deny that reality is fundamentally processive, nor can Christians deny—without appearing needlessly foolish—that even Christianity is historical. Therefore Christianity is only one among many ways of seeing, valuing, and interpreting reality-as-process. What is distinctive about Christian theology, a distinction it shares with Jewish thought, is its commitment to seeing or valuing this world-in-process as the creation of God. God continually creates by cease-lessly interacting with the whole created order. Indeed, if God were not so interacting there would be no creation-as-process. The world-as-creation is utterly dependent on God's ceaseless interactive pres-ence. This commitment to seeing or viewing the process as creation, while distinctive, is, of course, relative; it is only one of many historical ways—religious or scientific or philosophical—of viewing the flow which is reality.

The Christian *commitment* to reality as dependent on God's cre-ative activity is itself relative, that is, it is an historical *interpretation* of events. It is not the only possible interpretation. But the relativity of the commitment is not an argument against its truthfulness. As all modern theologians are aware, historical relativity and historical consciousness have made the truth question more interesting and more difficult, but not impossible.[40] Ever since Hume all thinkers concerned about truth are in the same relativistic boat. "Hume," writes Cobb, "discovered that the fundamental assumptions of both the science and the theology of his day derived from an interpretation of the data of experience which was not justified by the data them-selves."[41]

Theology, as Cobb and other process thinkers do it, should be seen as a conversation. On the one hand are Christians, committed to seeing or interpreting[42] the flow of events as creation. On the other hand are those who are committed to non-Christian and even nontheistic ways of envisioning and thus interpreting the same flow. Because process thinkers share a view of reality as becoming, they are obliged to challenge those theologians (and are challenged in return) who continue to tie Christian faith to what Cobb and others regard as an outmoded, even dangerous, view of reality, a view required neither by Scripture nor by modern modes of thought. So process theology continues to be a minority position. On the one wing of the continuum are those 20th-century theologians who to one degree or another reject the concept that all reality, including God, is becoming, processive, and relative. These theologians are convinced that Christian faith requires a fixed Ground (Tillich) or

Center (Gilkey)[43] or End (Pannenberg) or Revelation (Barth). Process theologians, however, also want to conduct a mutually critical conversation with thinkers on the other wing who are committed to an interpretation which denies that God is a necessary agent in everything that happens. Secularists and humanists, naturalists and materialists, and a whole host of others whose thought and practice are based on a fundamentally different (that is, nontheistic) interpretation of the historical flow of human and natural events make up those whose commitments are at odds with process theologians like John Cobb.

If all thinkers, not only process theologians but also those theologians to their right, as well as the humanists, secularists, and assorted nontheists and religious thinkers to their left, are in fact awash in the historical ebb and flow of a processive universe radically relativizing all events, even the way the most self-assured orthodox theologians think, then it is not difficult to answer the next question: What is the character of lostness within a world whose ultimate character is becoming?

Lostness as Chaos

It has often been remarked that process theologians do not write frequently of sin and evil. Some have suggested, quite wrongly, that process theology is incurably optimistic. The view of reality sketched above gives very little reason for optimism because, if nothing else, it highlights the risky, open, contingent, and haphazard character of events. John Cobb is very candid about how, as a university student, he experienced the "death" of God who had been conceived traditionally as the absolutely transcendent power in complete and perfect control of every detail of existence. Later, he "began to live into Whitehead's vision [of reality as organic and processive] which year by year became more my own."[44] For Cobb that has meant that God's relation to the world is not one of absolute control. God's way of ruling in the world involves God in sharing the world's risk and adventure. Therefore there is no absolute (that is, divine) guarantee that human beings, with limited but real freedom, will not use that freedom to destroy civilization through pollution, overpopulation, or a nuclear holocaust.[45] Sin is a function of

freedom in the human species. God does not control how that freedom is used nor does God interfere by sparing humans the consequences of their misuse of freedom. God may have the whole world
in God's hands, but it could blow up in God's hands too.

Chaos is a genuine possibility wherever, in the absence of absolute
divine control over every event, there are a multitude of creatures
each with a degree of real freedom. Even though the freedom is the
gift of God and thus "God has a certain responsibility for sin understood as the willful refusal of the best,"[46] God is not directly responsible for the decisions that are made in freedom.

The power which God exercises in the world is real and effective,
but cannot be compared to the "power required to lead an army of
tin soldiers." Every child has power, in that trivial sense of the term,
to overwhelm others with little power to resist.[47] To process theologians like Cobb it has been shocking that a favorite image of divine
power in traditional theology has been the trivial power of external
mechanical manipulation, or the power to coerce the will of another,
or the power that makes God responsible for everything that happens
in the exact way that it happens.

> When this view of God's omnipotence is combined with the Christian
> doctrine of man's accountability, there arises the monstrous idea that
> God's justice holds men responsible for sins even though God is him-
> self ultimately their author.[48]

The world lives under threat of chaos, but the ultimate threat is
not from God. Nor is it some known enemy or gigantic meteor
threatening to invade the earth from outer space. Nor has there
evolved on the earth a superior species of creature challenging the
dominion of humankind. Human beings themselves are the enemy,
and they alone are responsible for developing both the conditions
and the means of possible self-destruction—all of which is well
known. First, global pollution of air and water is making the earth
uninhabitable for more and more species of plants, birds, fish, and
all animal life, including humans. Second, overpopulation, over-
grazing, and the depletion of soil through irrigation and erosion have
steadily combined to induce regional shortages of food, resulting in
unprecedented starvation. Third, mutual fear between the two super-
powers continues to provoke the Russian and American governments

to escalate the nuclear arms buildup, which in turn diverts resources and energy away from decaying cities, a declining educational system, and the wounded environment.

There are several ways to view the possibility of a global catastrophe. One is the frequently held notion that God is in absolute control. Cobb, who is not alone in rejecting it, believes that this view can only hasten the disaster because it encourages passivity at best and at worst invites believers to welcome the apocalypse as desperate good news. It is a grotesque form of hope to propose that a nuclear holocaust is God's will and that, although humans will be held responsible for destroying God's gift of life on the earth, God can be counted on—not to save the earth and her "crown of creation"—but to forgive those who destroyed it all.

An alternative view is to regard the world in nontheistic terms, a view which gained ascendancy following the Enlightenment. For some time it has guided the way many people in Western societies deal with the natural order. Belief in God is confined strictly to the more or less private relationship between God and individuals. The God-world relation has diminished or disappeared. The consequence has usually been to "see" nature—the external world—simply as something to be used, consumed, and enjoyed. Its value is not "seen" in terms of its sacredness as a gift from God. Nature is thought to have value only to the degree that humans can use it for material gain or recreational pleasure. This attitude or way of "seeing" nature assumes that if a natural resource *can* be used— or even used up—as a means to the human ends of profit and/or pleasure, then it *ought* to be. Once the technological capacity for using a natural resource is available there is an assumed obligation to use it.

The scriptural vision—as a third possibility—calls humanity to be stewards of God's creation, and most especially of the earth and all its inhabitants. In some respects this view is closer to Asian philosophies and religions than to Western utilitarian attitudes. In most practical matters regarding the environment, however, stewardship has not guided public policy. Rather, a more utilitarian and human-centered view has guided public policy and now hastens the deterioration of the planet's capacity to sustain life. Meanwhile, Christians seem to be of a double mind regarding the environment upon which human existence depends. Even though the Scriptures do not encourage such double-mindedness, many Christians apparently have found it possible in their thinking to accept *both* the destructive (and largely Western) view of nature as a mere thing to be used (rather than as God's creation to be cared for by responsible stewards) *and* the view that God is the omnipotent ruler who causes all things to happen just as they happen. In combination these two views turn Christians into passive collaborators in what could eventually be the destruction of humanity.

Process theologians like John Cobb have for some time argued that Christians need to reconsider—and to reformulate—certain basic ideas about God and the world,[49] and that this reformulation must be done in relative independence of the specific Christian revelation of Jesus as the Christ. It is obvious from the foregoing description of lostness as chaos threatening the created order that this reformulation would have implications for how one eventually speaks of Christ. As with other 20th-century theologians, the prior sense of the human predicament also shapes how process theologians develop their understanding of Jesus as Savior.

Jesus: The Christ as Creative Transformation

Unless humanity can be persuaded to give up certain dangerous habits of thought and action, the earth may well be overwhelmed by the destructive chaos unleashed upon nature and the civilized world by the misguided intelligence of humans. It is out of that profound moral concern that Cobb has proposed a different way to think about the world. The earth is like a doomed ship in the sea of the universe. It is not certain that it *will* be saved, but Cobb believes that it certainly *can* be saved. It is in danger because its best educated and most privileged passengers, by their selfish misuse of resources, have fomented revolt among those in steerage. The engineers have so neglected ship maintenance that it is about to sink, and its officers squabble among themselves over authority of command.[50] To hope for some *deus ex machina* is to hope in vain and can only postpone rectifying the situation. Someone on board must start thinking and acting differently and stimulate common thought and action. Wishful thinking and hocus-pocus action are useless.

The future of the earth and all its passenger-inhabitants depends on thought and action which can transform it from a doomed vessel adrift in the universe to a safe, peaceful, and harmonious community of travelers. For Cobb, such thought and action means a break not only with traditional concepts of God and the world but also with modernity's dominant modes of thought and action.

The greatest danger comes from thinking that the future has already been determined either by events in the past or by a pre-recorded master program which needs only to unwind from the reel of eternity and pass moment by moment through the time machine called Now. Therefore it is urgent that people start thinking differently. The future is only partially but not fully determined by past circumstances. If the future were fully determined by what has already happened it would only mean inertia, entropy, and decay. If the future were fully determined by an Absolute Mind, then that same Mind, because it has also and already fully determined the present dangerous situation just as it is, must be a monster Mind torturing us with illusions.

Contrary to images of the future as mostly deterministic,[51] Cobb accepts a view of the future as open, contingent, and full of possibilities never available previously. "Our hope for the future is based on the unpredictability of that future, that is, its partial undeterminedness." While other thinkers may regard an open future as the negation of hope, Cobb seizes on the unpredictability of the future as the basis for developing a theology of hope. A genuinely open future means that humans can still be transformed and can yet turn the world away from the self-destructive course upon which humanity has steered it in the first place. That means that we must hoist a different banner, we must think and act differently. We must stop projecting on to the future deterministic and destructive images even if those images have had an honored place in the Christian tradition. "We need a unifying image to guide us in our hopeful openness to being transformed. Christ provides such an image. . . ."[52]

Some images of Christ, however, do not unify or help but only burden and paralyze believers with conceptions of the future as already settled. Cobb proposes a different image: Christ must be "imaged" as the one who himself breaks old forms, questions familiar conceptions, relativizes conventional patterns, challenges every expectation, and qualifies every traditional interpretation. When our favorite Christological definitions crumble under the pressure of new circumstances, it is Christ himself who breaks the definitions by which we would claim some relation with Christ. Christ relativizes all our commitments, even to our most cherished traditions, in order that we might be transformed. Creative transformation is a pervasive feature of human history, a feature which Cobb illustrates by using Malraux's history of art—and without that pervasive feature history would be decay and nothing but decay. In Christ all received values and images are relativized, *including* traditional images of Christ. "To identify Christ with the new is to see the new as unrealized potentiality for transforming the world without destroying it."[53]

Cobb thus redefines Christ as the principle of creative transformation who, while everywhere at work, is not uniformly effective everywhere. For example, the effectiveness of Christ often is thwarted even by Christians who will not allow Christ to break them free of their favorite Christologies, but instead huddle in isolation apart from where Christ is at work making all things new. Indeed,

> Christian consciousness must be freed from its fear that to move forward in the acceptance of the secular and pluralistic world threatens its faithfulness to Christ. The secular consciousness [also!] must be freed from its fear that to acknowledge its own positive principle as Christ will be a betrayal of its critical and open spirit. The pluralistic consciousness [as well!] must be freed from its fear that to name Christ as universal is to close itself to the independent power and truth of other traditions. The thesis . . . is that faithfulness to Christ requires immersion in the secular and pluralistic consciousness and that it is precisely there that Christ now works, impeded by our failure to recognize him and by our continuing association of faith with past, particularized expressions of Christ.[54]

Cobb believes that "creative transformation" is a more apt term than other images which no longer are able "to give a post-Western culture, now global, the courage to struggle against the patterns of self-destruction that now control it."[54] Tillich, for the sake of fidelity to the reality of Christ, rejected traditional images of salvation which no longer express their original intention. Cobb similarly proposes a new way of speaking of Christ in order that the always and every-where present reality of Christ can be more effective. Christians must have the courage to acknowledge that traditional images have died, that the cultural circumstances and conceptual framework in which they were formulated are in the past, and that new conceptual wineskins are now required, lest the ever-new wine of salvation be denied to this present and sorely threatened generation. Cobb believes that "apart from Christ there is no hope," which is tantamount to saying that if the dynamic, creative, salvific power of Christ as creative transformation were removed from the world there would only be "the running down of the world governed by slow inertial decay."[56]

Of course, the reality of Christ is never absent (it is, after all, an ontological reality) and so creative transformation will always be (one might say) God's way of sustaining creation. So why name Jesus as the explicit, historical instance or incarnation of the hidden Christ? For Cobb the special—indeed the missionary—urgency for naming Jesus as the Christ is that "apart from the history of Jesus, hope is distorted and Christ's effective presence is blocked."[57]

According to the Christian doctrine of preexistence, Christ as the Logos was a necessary factor in the world prior to the birth of Jesus of Nazareth. "He [Christ] is the image of the invisible God, the first-born of all creation; for in him all things were created, in heaven and on earth, visible and invisible . . . all were created through him and for him. He is before all things" (Col. 1:15ff.). Even if Jesus had never been born, and certainly before he was born, the Christ or "creative transformation," as Cobb choses to speak of Christ, was a present, necessary, and universal power.

In effect, Cobb believes that the Christ has always been and will always be effective throughout the whole universe. On *earth,* however, there are humans peculiarly endowed with limited but real freedom and with limited but, nevertheless, exceptional intelligence. On earth the *effectiveness* of the Christ, as creative transformation, can be impeded or even overwhelmed by humanity's misuse of its freedom and intelligence. On earth the human species threatens to inflict on the ecosphere an unimaginable and catastrophic loss of value. Even though that loss would be mostly confined to the planet earth, it would be real and tragic, all the more so because it is neither inevitable nor necessary.

One might say, then, that Jesus is the special, divine concession granted for the salvation of the human family who has put the earth and itself in jeopardy. Only if the Christ—the always and everywhere present power of creative transformation—takes particular human form can the salvific function of Christ effectively turn humanity away from self-destruction and establish a worldwide community of humans who live at peace among themselves and in harmony with the environment on which all life depends. Only if humans can be thus saved from destructive modes of thought and action can the God-world relation be restored as well. It is only in human form that the saving power of God can break through to human beings and thus have a chance of turning the human race away from self-afflicted disaster. And so Jesus is the historical or incarnational channel by means of which the always and everywhere present Logos as creative transformation had to be specifically beamed precisely at humanity, whose demonic misuse of intelligence and inventiveness threatens the future of the earth and its inhabitants.[58]

Our brief sketches of the Christologies of Paul Tillich and of John Cobb have focused on the theme of this book, namely, the question of salvation. The manner in which each of them constructs a Christology is shaped by the prior sense of what threatens human existence. The emphasis in each case has been on the relation of God and world. Even though worldviews change from age to age, these theologians do not believe it possible or desirable for Christian thinkers to avoid demonstrating how the truth confessed by Christians is related to the truth discerned by other thinkers and investigators. The Christ who is proclaimed in a variety of ways by the churches is also the Christ who is hidden in every nook and cranny of reality which is, after all, the creation of God.[59]

Chapter Four

THE SAVIOR
AS LIBERATOR
AND AS RECONCILER

The historical situation is that two-thirds of humanity are subject to dependence and domination. Thirty million people a year die of hunger and malnutrition. That situation must become the starting point for any Christian theology today, even in the dominant, affluent countries. Otherwise theology will not be able to situate and concretize its basic themes in history. Its questions will not be real questions, for they will bypass real human beings.[1]

This statement by one of the Latin American liberation theologians announces the most controversial program within the church, especially within the Roman Catholic communion, and the most publicized of theological movements. It has been featured in weekly magazines, radio, television, and major newspapers. Its leading authors have been called to Rome to defend their published views before the authorities of the Vatican, and their views have been criticized by the pope when he visited Latin America. Thus liberation theology is a public theology both in the sense that its leading figures have become celebrities outside the church press and that its adherents believe that theology ought to influence public policies and practices which are unjust and oppressive and not confine itself to the institutional church or to matters of strictly private morality. Liberation theologians break the conventional barrier of silence between religion and politics.

Most of the theologians of the movement would agree with the the opening quotation and would doubtless be joined by their counterparts in Africa, and by the women, black, and Hispanic theologians of North America.[2] Although no reputable theologian intentionally advocates a theology that would "bypass real human beings," liberation theologians have charged that in practice the work of many highly regarded academic theologians does just that: it may be intellectually credible in its *explanation* of the Christian faith but it fails to make any difference in the urgently needed *transformation* of the political and social conditions which hold multitudes of God's people in dehumanizing oppression and domination. For instance, the much-celebrated controversy in Great Britain over the so-called myth of the incarnation[3] or the earlier debate provoked by Bishop J. A. T. Robinson's book, *Honest To God,* while very much in the public view, did not have any discernible impact on public policy in England nor did anyone expect or seek such an influence.

The agreement among liberation theologians about the starting place, however, must not be taken to mean that they merely extrapolate a theology from sociological and political studies of male domination over women, or of capitalist domination over Third World nations, or of white domination over blacks and Native Americans. Sociopolitical analyses do not of themselves produce theology, and every liberation theologian presumes that to be the case. While they are clear that the starting point for theology is the human situation of oppression and injustice, they are just as clear that it is as *theologians* that they give their prior attention to oppression of people throughout the world. They—of course—believe in God who is the *theos* of their theology but they insist that the *logos* of theology, that is, theology's thinking and speaking, must be fashioned out of the matrix of human suffering. There is more at stake here than method or style. It is not unusual for a theologian's manner (of speaking, thinking, and acting) to alter the matter (God, world, and self) about which any theologian is by definition concerned. Before attending to the matter of liberation theology, specifically its Christology, it is necessary to comment on certain features of its methodology.

Principles of Method in Liberation Theology

1. Theology as the second step

Gustavo Gutiérrez, who is among the most widely recognized of the liberation theologians, declared in *A Theology of Liberation* that theology ought to be the "second step" and not the first which a Christian should take. By proposing that theology be relieved of the obligation to take the first step, Guttiérrez predicted that believers, especially Christian pastors, would thereby be freed from the compulsion of having first of all to get their theology in perfect order before they could act or speak on behalf of oppressed people. When theology is the first step Christians must take, then they are too much inclined to restrict themselves to the tradition and to speak and act only out of that tradition or to speak and to act only within the boundaries of the church, as though Christian activity can only flow from presumably approved theological premises. Theology, when construed as the first step, confines and restricts, but when construed as the second step it liberates and is itself liberated.

> Theology is reflection, a critical attitude. Theology *follows*. What Hegel used to say about philosophy can likewise be applied to theology; it rises only at sundown. . . . Instead of using only revelation and tradition as starting points, as classical theology has generally done, it must start with facts and questions derived from the world and from history.[4]

If theology were to surrender the dubious privilege of being the first step, and instead were to follow, that is, were to wait until the end of the day and only then reflect critically on Christian action in the world, there would be liberation. Such liberation might operate in several directions. First, Christians would be liberated *from* the tyranny of theology which holds them captive in the church. Second, they would be liberated *for* dealing with the facts and questions as those facts and questions would emerge and are encountered in the world. Third, theology itself would be liberated *from* the burden of anticipating and supervising every aspect of Christian life, as has been too often the case when the church uses theology to suppress its own members and to keep them subservient to the political order, thus cooperating with the dominant civil authorities in maintaining an unjust social system.[5] Fourth, theology would be liberated *for* its own proper role of

> sinking roots where the pulse of history is beating this moment and illuminating history with the Word of the Lord of history, who irreversibly committed himself to the present moment of mankind to carry it to its fulfillment. . . . [Theology of liberation, then, is] not so much a new theme for reflection as a *new way* to do theology. Theology as critical reflection on historical praxis [or pastoral activity] is a liberating theology, a theology of liberating transformation. . . . This is a theology which does not stop with reflecting on the world, but rather tries to be part of the process through which the world is transformed.[6]

When theology is truly "part of the process through which the world is transformed" it is carried out differently than has been typical of most theological work. It is more open-ended, more involved in a continuing conversation than in reaching conclusions or in securing and defending fixed positions. It abandons its fortress mentality and moves out into the open. Because it is not a "school" led by a major figure like a Barth or a Tillich but is a shared responsibility, no one figure is looked to as the definitive authority. In addition, because it is a new way of critically reflecting upon activity in the public realm, liberation theology is always adapting and correcting itself. North American women, for instance, have challenged Latin American males for ignoring the oppression of women, and Native Americans like Vine Deloria have charged that liberation theologians are still too attached to Western ways of dealing with a problem.

Very significantly—for many of its adherents—this "new way" of doing theology is carried on as much outside the academy as within the halls of research and teaching, and so the key word of the movement is *praxis,* already in danger of becoming a slogan. *Praxis* is perhaps best defined as engaged or involved thinking rather than mere cogitation or speculation far removed from the day-by-day struggle to change the world and make it more livable and humane.[7]

2. Jesus and Marxist philosophy

It is well known that liberation theologians make extensive use of Marxist philosophy. As theologians, of course, they are not alone in using philosophical systems which have been worked out independently of Christian faith.[8] But inasmuch as Marxism is not only an atheistic system of thought which is deeply critical of religion, but is also the official philosophy which informs large political systems like those of Russia and of the People's Republic of China, it is not surprising that when theologians use Marxist thought they attract the suspicion of the pope, whose native Poland has been brutalized by communism, and of Western Christians, many of whom to some degree or other believe that certain forms of capitalism are genuinely beneficial to most people.[9]

Passions usually run very deep whenever religion and politics or Christianity and communism are brought together; therefore it has been difficult for Latin American liberationists to be heard. One of them, Juan Luis Segundo, has especially argued that Christian faith and Marxist philosophy do not contradict but complement one another. One of his stratagems is to define "religion" in such a way that, if they were to accept it, Christians would have no need to defend Christian faith against Marx's attack on religion. In simplest terms, Segundo rejects theological and anthropological definitions of religion—specifically referring to those offered by David Tracy and Clifford Geertz—and instead he refers to Jesus for his definition of religion, prompted in part by the well-known book by Milan Machovec, *A Marxist Looks at Jesus.*[10] Segundo, the Christian, joins Machovec, the Marxist, in recognizing approvingly the essential rightness of Jesus' sharp polemics against religion.

As Segundo reads the Gospels, the most important criterion by which "religion" should be judged is not its professed creed or doctrine but whether or not it serves human welfare. All religions, without exception, are historical and relative. Religion is not an absolute requirement for life; many people live worthwhile lives with no apparent religious commitment. Caring for the welfare of other humans, on the other hand, is such a requirement if humanity is to survive. "The sabbath was made for man, not man for the sabbath" (Mark 2:27). Of course it is the case that while most religions point to God, Marxism denies God. How, then, can there be any factor of complementarity between Jesus and Marx? Segundo merely reminds his readers that while "everything of a 'religious nature' points to God . . ., the God of Jesus, paradoxically enough, points to human beings, their needs and their values."[11] And that, of course, is what Marxism at its best also points to. Marx—like Jesus—sharply criticized religion for its failure to attend to what is the absolute obligation for all humans: the needs of the neighbor.

If the neighbor's needs and values are what are absolutely binding on every person, then it is clear that theology's task is not to defend religion against Marx, but to reflect critically on what sort of action is most likely to serve the neighbor in authentic ways. Ultimately, the Christian will have a dispute with the atheistic Marxist about what is the highest good for the neighbor; after all, just how is salvation related to liberation?[12] But the Christian who follows Jesus cannot dispute Jesus' admonition that whatever that good might turn out to be, it is never to be determined by criteria imposed from an outside religious authority; it is never forced on or into human beings "for their own good." Rather, the criteria for determining the good are found in the human, not outside the human. "Whatever goes into a man from outside cannot defile him. . . . What comes out of a man is what defiles a man" (Mark 7:18f.; Matt. 15:11). For Segundo this means that "only the projects of human beings make them pure or impure, moral or immoral." The criteria of the good are human, not "religious," and if one were to ask what is human, Segundo would reply that only humans can answer that, not religious authorities. "In other words, one's understanding of the human being is prior to, and independent of religious prescriptions."[13]

3. The historical Jesus

This very preliminary grasp on the method of liberation theology, specifically its use of Marxism, leads to another major feature of the way this theology works. Instead of appealing to authoritative doctrine about Christ first of all, it appeals to the historical example of the life of Jesus, which in turns authorizes the primary importance of praxis. In other words, the first step is not to ask what is religiously or even doctrinally permissible but, prompted by Jesus, to ask which actions are most suitable for helping the neighbor.[14] Marxist social analysis, so the liberation argument goes, is a helpful diagnostic tool for discerning the systemic causes of injustice, poverty, and abuse of natural resources, and therefore is a great help in posing the questions of the first step. The motivation for adopting any means for helping the neighbor is faithfulness to Jesus. The community of faith is free, in principle, to consider a variety of means, and then, after critical theological reflection has investigated the facts and the questions encountered in the first step, is also free to choose whichever means are the most effective. So long as the means do not violate the criterion which is absolutely binding on those who follow Jesus, "religious" objections can be disregarded. As one liberationist has put it, "The New Testament is unanimous: Salvation has already appeared and calls itself Jesus Christ; he is the new humanity, the first to arrive at the goal; we will follow him."[15]

For many liberation theologians, then, the historical Jesus is the one by whose authority theology is demoted to the second step, while Marxist sociopolitical analysis is adopted as the tool for the first step, namely, taking the measure of the neighbors' needs.

4. The kingdom of God

A further methodological comment is that the kingdom of God, central to the preaching of Jesus, is practically the sole hermeneutical principle for understanding the ministry of the historical Jesus and for relating Jesus to the political context today. Jesus announced and inaugurated God's kingdom, and in the light of that promised reign of God all political systems are relativized. Therefore, to believe in the coming kingdom of God means that no earthly system can command the total allegiance of believing citizens because their faith has freed them from expecting that any political scheme can ultimately save them. Followers of Jesus should always be suspicious of political and religious systems because they serve primarily the special interests of the few and have little concern for the welfare of all God's people. A "hermeneutic of suspicion" will guide their interpretation of every system. In that sense Christians are revolutionary, because their faith is set upon a different order: the coming kingdom of God. Believers in the kingdom know that no matter what the present system is, it is neither necessary nor willed by God. Gutiérrez writes, "An unjust situation does not happen by chance; it is not . . . a fatal destiny; there is human responsibility behind it."[16]

Liberation theologians, then, call for action. If present systems of injustice are the result of human responsibility, then humans can also take responsibility for changing them. It is in light of the coming kingdom of God, and by the authority of Jesus' own life and preaching, that liberation theologians enlist the victims of injustice, not as zealots for "political-religious messianism," but as agents who work to eliminate oppression for the sake of the neighbor. Again, Gutiérrez: "The future of history belongs to the poor and exploited. True liberation will be the work of the oppressed themselves; in them, the Lord saves history." [17]

At least for Latin American liberationists, then, there are the following major elements which make this theology a "new way" but not a new faith. Instead of trying to reinterpret and explain doctrine in order to make it more academically acceptable, this theology seeks to re-position believers so that their action makes a real difference and transforms the human situation. Instead of using Aristotle, Hegel, existentialism, or process philosophy, this theology uses the philosophy of Marx, not merely to "explain" but to analyze the human situation and develop methods of transforming it. Instead of beginning with high doctrines of revelation or proofs of resurrection, this theology begins with the historical Jesus. And instead of emphasizing first of all the person of Christ as the perfect union of humanity and divinity (to be sure, liberationists do affirm the dogmatic formulations, but not as their most urgent first task) this theology first of all emphasizes the preaching and the action of Jesus. By centering on the kingdom of God, Jesus in his own preaching and teaching relativized all earthly authority and was thus critical of both civil and cultic systems at the point where they failed to serve human welfare; his kingdom-centered criticism quite naturally provoked the opposition of religious and political authorities who conspired to have him crucified.

Lostness as Oppression

In these chapters we are analyzing various Christologies according to the dimensions of lostness which are presupposed by each of them. Throughout this investigation lostness has been so understood and defined that it *not* refer primarily to subjective feelings, human desires, or selfish wants—or even to political biases, although feelings and biases are not irrelevant to lostness. As used in these chapters *lostness* is primarily a theological term and takes its fundamental meaning from the structure which defines the very nature of theology: the essential relatedness of God, world, and self. What is lost is the relationship *as God intended it to be.*

Of all human disciplines, theology alone seeks to make clear to the mind and to defend against its detractors the truth of faith's claim that the world and humanity are upheld in an essential relationship with God, a relationship without which they could not exist, and that it is God who alone and absolutely determines that relationship. God's will, so goes faith's claim, is unique and absolute in the sense that it is not dependent on anything else. Thus, it is out of God's absolute self-determination (God freely and alone determines God's being) that God calls forth and sustains the creation, which in turn is constituted by the indissoluble relationship of God, self, and world.

The *theological* meaning of the term *lostness,* then, is derived from what theology is all about: God, world, and self, whose essential relatedness (as intended by God) has been tragically ruptured, profoundly disjoined, and broken by sin. Lostness, theologically understood, means that the essential relatedness of God, world, and self has been marred beyond human ability to repair it. All the king's horses and all the king's men cannot put together again what has been broken by the Fall. Like Humpty Dumpty, the essential relatedness has been broken, but the relatedness itself has not been destroyed or obliterated, because that relatedness, while broken, is seen, theologically, still bound to the fixed will of God. Even though God's *will* to be who God will be—namely, the God who holds Godself and world and humanity in relatedness—has not been shaken, *what* God wills (the relationship itself) has been spoiled beyond human ability to repair it. Only when lostness is seen against the background of God's unbendable will (God is determined to remain in relationship with God's creation broken by the Fall) does the full depth and mystery of sin come into view. The mystery of sin has its chief source in the mystery of God and God's will: Why does God faithfully and generously choose to be bound to a rebellious humanity in a fallen creation?

In this chapter we are considering those Christologies which emphasize lostness primarily as brokenness within the *self-world* relationship, just as previous chapters analyzed Christologies which have focused on the human predicament primarily in terms of the *God-self* polarity (Barth and Pannenberg) or the *God-world* polarity (Tillich and Cobb). The self-world relation, because it seems to make no immediate or *explicit* reference to God (however *implicit* God's relation may be) is naturally open to an unlimited variety of interpretations. The self's sojourn in the world and interaction with the world are topics on which theologians certainly have no monopoly. There is scarcely a form of art, science, or philosophy, or any mode of political or economic activity which does not disclose directly or indirectly one or more aspects of human selves and their variously troubled relationship with the world. What distinguishes theology from other forms of discourse about this relationship is theology's insistence that, however brilliant or insightful or penetrating other forms of discourse about humanity-in-the-world may be, such speaking can never be adequate to the full reality of that relationship or to the tragic elements of the human, until and unless the experience of humanity-in-the-world is comprehended in God.

Theology, by implication, then, claims that all other modes of thought and discourse, such as sociology or psychology or ecology, regardless of how true they may be in most other respects, are nevertheless inadequate. This claim has always made theologians especially susceptible to charges of intellectual arrogance. So quick to spot the nontheological, and therefore allegedly inadequate, bias of other disciplines, theologians are especially prone to being blind to their own biases. Liberation theology in some respects avoids that tendency, because it does not insist that a theological interpretation of the self-world relation has priority over other interpretations. Liberation theology waits its turn, and only then takes the "second step." Liberation theologians do not typically engage in the apologetic task of arguing for the theological interpretation of reality.[18] As already noted, these theologians begin neither with explicit theological arguments nor with dogmatic assertions about God and the world, or God and the self. They insist, instead, that theology must be grounded first of all in actual experiences of the brokenness of human action in the world and not in the abstractions of thought and logic.[19]

Lostness, then, when viewed along the self-world polarity, takes many forms, but all of them are open to public knowledge because, quite simply, they belong to the world of history and experience. The mystery of sin in its ultimate depth may be hidden (except to the eyes of faith glimpsing some aspect of the terrifying transcendence of God), but the forms of lostness are part of the visible, public reality of human beings in their distorted relation to each other and to the social and natural environment in which they live and on which they depend for their existence.[20]

The predominant characteristic of distorted relationships, as liberation theologians insist, is oppression. Oppression so disturbs the relationships which God intends for mutual support, for cooperation, for symbiotic enrichment, and for growth, that they deteriorate into what can best be described as zero-sum systems. That is, God intends that relationships through mutuality and cooperation will ideally build up and enrich all the members, but in an oppressive system only some of the members gain, and always at the expense of the others. When the losses of the oppressed are subtracted from the gains of the oppressors, the result is zero. In oppressive systems all sustain a loss simply because the cost in energy, time, and resources for maintaining the mechanisms which oppression requires is a drain on every member of the system. This is most apparent in a totalitarian police state, which is necessarily committed to maintaining censorship, guarding sealed borders, and restraining dissident members of the society. The cost for such measures deprives everyone. Similar observations could be made of families in which the head of the family, with harsh enforcement, demands above all else strict and total obedience. Whatever satisfactions the family elders may realize from achieving strict order is far less than the short-term cost of enforcement and the probable long-term loss of having the younger members fail to grow into the freedom and responsibility of adulthood. Even when a family is permissive and accommodating to a child or to an alcoholic adult, it allows that member to dominate and thus to oppress others. That, too, is a zero-sum system.

Social systems which do not achieve mutuality and cooperation among their members, but instead encourage exploitation and domination, cannot survive, and in actuality threaten other societies because they diminish but do not replenish, consume but do not create, the resources which benefit life in relationship.

For liberationists in Latin America, economic forms of oppression are tantamount to political forms. These theologians have been especially critical of the failure of civil, military, and economic leaders to provide for the well-being of all citizens in a safe, just, and harmonious society. Those with such power too often serve only the interests and the advantage of the privileged few. The theologians charge that military and political leaders conspire with business and economic interests to exploit and oppress the poor. By failing to bind all citizens together, and by serving primarily the special interests of an elite, governments actually foster animosity between people along the lines of economic class. The lower economic classes who live in such societies have neither the power nor the freedom to alter the system which, in effect, holds them in bondage.[21]

Because the oppressive use of economic power is central to any discussion of liberation theology in the context of the so-called Third World nations, a brief comment about economics is in order here. In the developed, and largely capitalist, countries, the freedom to accumulate capital and private property is an especially important right. But according to the Marxist view the accumulation of private wealth goes against human nature; for a Marxist, private wealth is the equivalent of original sin. Just as the personal right to accumulate wealth is close to the center of a capitalist view of life, in the Marxist view it is contrary to the best interests of being human because it disturbs not only personal relationships among humans but also upsets their relationship with nature. Human beings are members of an ecosystem, the optimum functioning of which depends on co-operation among persons and between humans and nature. As an organic whole the ecosystem has its own metabolism, and that metabolism, like the functioning of one's body, is so complex that any local disturbance upsets the whole system. It goes against the nature of humanity to disturb the metabolism by which humanity is sustained.

Humans are critically important members of the ecosystem; its metabolism requires that in their labor and social interaction, humans assume responsibility for the care of nature. It requires also that their dominion over nature have the positive purpose of fulfilling *all* life, human *and* natural. But the accumulation of capital, based as it is on self-interest, goes against the broader best interest of all people and their natural environment as well. Thus, acquisition of private wealth disturbs the homeostatic and metabolic relationship, and promotes instead the rise of a whole capitalist class which removes itself from direct involvement in the metabolism of labor. It does not cooperatively interact with nature, and is thus alienated not only from nature but from those who are more immediately involved with and more directly dependent on nature. Furthermore, in the ecosystem any living creature, even when it is alienated from any part of the system, is still dependent on the homeostasis of the system. Therefore, the alienation of any class of members from the whole on which all are dependent is dangerous for all. There can be no genuine health, no fulfillment, no productivity for humanity when the ecosystem—the human reality at its broadest and deepest—is dominated by noncooperative, parasitic members who, even while dominating the system by accumulating wealth, derive their power from it by extracting wealth for themselves without contributing to the life of the whole.

As envisioned in Marxist thought, capital, because it is based on self-interest, simply goes against reality and thus disturbs the homeostatic system. The inevitable consequence is a large dependent underclass who have poor housing, nutrition, education, and health care. Typically, the system will also encourage the exploitation of nature for profit with the usual result of extensive pollution of the environment.[22]

It is fairly obvious that this Marxist criticism of belief in the right to accumulate capital is itself based on a certain vision or faith.[23] The Marxist envisions the true nature of all life as an ecosystem of mutual interdependence among all participants. When, in this view, humans act out of self-interest rather than out of interest for the whole, the result is oppressive to both self and world—that is, to the ecosystem both in its natural and its human aspects. It is also fairly obvious why liberation theologians, for whom lostness as oppression is first of all a theological term, would find much that is valuable in this Marxist vision.

Finally, mention must be made of racist and sexist oppression. Black theologians as well as women theologians in North America are certainly part of the movement of liberation theology, but they represent distinct types. Like Latin American theologians, they also begin with the concrete experience of oppression and go on to insist that their own experience of living in North America as blacks, women, Native Americans, or Hispanics gives them a different and legitimate perspective from which to view the Christian tradition.

From the base of their different experiences they return to the biblical witness and to the history of the church and find in those sources authorization for a reinterpretation of Jesus. For example, James Cone finds it permissible to say that Jesus is black. Elizabeth Fiorenza uncovers biblical evidence that Jesus began a movement in which women from the very beginning had equal responsibility, an equality only later denied them when the church adopted the oppressive style of the larger society. Contemporary scholars like these argue that the New Testament witness to Jesus has been distorted because authority in the church has been concentrated in the hands of a white male elite who, against the clear testimony of Scripture and contrary to Jesus' ministry, have oppressed women and non-Europeans by denying them freedom and equality.[24]

Jesus as Liberator

That Jesus is Savior as liberator has been the contention most especially of Leonardo Boff, a Brazilian theologian, whose work has stirred considerable controversy in the Roman Catholic community. He notes that while most of the titles ascribed to Jesus have come from liturgical and sacred sources, some others are secular, for example, Christ as the head of the cosmos. Boff thinks that theologians must find appropriate secular names which can reveal who Jesus is for this age. No title for Jesus should ever be absolutized, either the ancient and revered ones or the secular and popular ones.

Any title for Jesus that is drawn from secular sources will reflect the worldview of its time or *saeculum*. In the present day, the evolutionist view of reality is more and more taken for granted, so Christ can be spoken of as the Omega Point, the absolute within history toward which the entire evolutionary process is moving and in which (whom?) it finds its goal. This secular title is intended to express, in terms fit for this age, what the primitive Christian community meant by asserting that in Christ God is already all in all (1 Cor. 15:28). Boff proposes that other secular titles would be appropriate in light of contemporary viewpoints and that no title should be rejected merely because it reflects a "secular" viewpoint.

For intellectuals in affluent societies, the preferred conceptual world is evolutionist. For the vast majority of human beings the real world is one of hunger, poverty, and disease. Meanwhile, the gap between the affluent minority and poor majority increases world-wide. Communication techniques make the poor more and more aware of that gap. The consequence is a highly explosive global situation, ripe for any revolutionary change that might offer some relief for the poor and the oppressed. Therefore, if Christ as the Omega Point is a secular title fit for an evolutionary consciousness, then Christ as the Liberator is a secular title fit for a revolutionary consciousness. Boff writes:

> Christ is held in high regard by many and followed as a dissenter, a liberator, a reformer, a revolutionary. . . . However, we should not confuse the terms. . . . It is not liberation from Roman subjugation, nor a shout of rebellion by the poor against Jewish landowners. It is total and complete liberation from all that alienates human beings, including sickness, death, and especially sin. The kingdom of God [which Jesus preached] cannot be reduced to a single dimension of the world.[25]

Boff here makes it clear that while liberation theologiàns are intent on detecting the saving work of Jesus in public and even political issues, the secular title *Liberator* as they use it is not confined to a single issue or "single dimension." Boff refuses to shrink the rel-evance of Christ to the individual's spiritual and family life, or to ecclesiastical and cultic activity, but wants to show how the work of Christ makes a difference in the public domain where the public dimensions of oppression are experienced. In that public domain theology will always insist on "God's preference for the poor and oppressed," a preference which is enunciated in the Old Testament prophets and embodied in the praxis, life, and teachings of Jesus.

How is salvation as liberation in the public realm to be articulated? Again, for Boff, the kingdom of God is the guiding theme. Jesus in his ministry did not focus on himself or on the church but on the coming kingdom of God which he, by his life and teachings, in-augurated. When the kingdom of God comes it means "a restruc-turing of the human world."[26] Although it is always God who ini-tiates these changes in the human situation they can take effect only if people are first of all converted. And so Jesus as Liberator is the one who frees people by converting them *from* their oppressed consciousness (here is where the Marxist analysis of economic alienation is useful) and liberates them *for* love and spontaneity and liberty. In Boff's words, ". . . if Christ liberates the human person from the laws, he does not hand people over to libertarianism or irresponsibility. Rather he creates even stronger bonds and ties than those of the law. Love must bind all people among themselves." Christ's liberation from oppressive legalism and social convention does not mean freedom to do as one pleases but it does mean freedom to do good for the neighbor. Jesus liberates his followers to achieve what the law fails to accomplish: the genuine well-being of all people. [27]

Second, Jesus "announces a fundamental equality: All are worthy of love. . . . All are children of the same Father and because of this are brothers and sisters." [28] For anyone who lives at the bottom of the socioeconomic scale, equality is radical good news because it means that social class as well as the ecclesiastical and political pyramids or hierarchies of authority are broken up by Jesus' announcement of equality. "Thus liberation christology . . . is truly liberative because it implies a break with the status quo." [29] It takes the side of the oppressed; it looks at society from the bottom up and does not wait for the elite to send help from above by some "trickle down" theory. Rather than accepting and looking for help from the structures of economic or political power at the top, it challenges the entire social ethos by which inequities of class, economics, and politics are sanctified and protected, often with the consent of church authorities. It is this oppressive and widespread ethos whose grip on the minds of all economic classes holds the poor in bondage. Jesus' announcement of an all-embracing equality becomes, then, the basis for Christians to challenge this ethos.

Third, Jesus is Liberator because the kingdom of God which Jesus initiated "implies a revolution of the human world." If all people in reality (that is, in the kingdom of God) are equal, then the present social order of unequal classes, races, and nationalities is against reality and must change. "The present order of things cannot save people from their fundamental alienation," which has its roots in the misuse of power. "A change of life is required, a complete turnabout of the old situation." Jesus is Liberator because the kingdom of God, God's way of ruling in the world, "secularizes the principle of authority." In God's kingdom authority is reversed from a function of privilege to a function of service so that wherever God's way of ruling prevails, all notions of authority as the privilege of the elite must be abandoned and a new order installed. Jesus said, "Whoever would be great among you must be your servant, and whoever would be first among you must be your slave" (Matt. 20:27).[30]

Finally, the distinction between neighbor and stranger no longer exists. The kingdom of God implies that no family, race, nation, or social class can have priority in the Christian's loyalty. "According to this new vision, the Christian does not belong to any family, but to the family of the whole world. All people are the Christian's brothers and sisters." In Jesus the transnational vision called the kingdom of God overcomes the profound alienations which have encrusted humanity and its history. By initiating that kingdom "Jesus [the Liberator] gave people back to themselves." Boff recalls that the philosopher Celsus considered the early Christians dangerous— even revolutionary—not because Christians directly attacked the status quo but "because they were in favor of indiscriminate love, for pagans, Christians, barbarians, Romans and because they unmasked the imperial ideology that made the Emperor a God and the structures of the vast Empire something divine." Because Christians believe that the kingdom of God transcends all alienating loyalties, they can often be perceived as different and even revolutionary. The early Christians not only indiscriminately welcomed Jews, Gentiles, Romans, Greeks, slave, free, rich, and poor but also asserted that for them what determined good or bad, divine or diabolic, religious or irreligious was "what is revealed in the heart that opens itself to God and to others." The comportment of these people "provoked in the Roman Empire a non-violent social revolution." Jesus the Liberator was the one who so affected people that they dreamed of a kingdom "which is not an entirely different world but this world completely new and renewed."[31]

In Boff's view, liberation neither happens all by itself nor does Jesus accomplish it by fiat, all by himself. Jesus the Liberator needs followers in order to actualize liberation first by proclamation of the kingdom which is coming and second by trying to change the world. There are things that can be done to liberate. "Hence there must be differences in the way we organize love and justice in society." The third imperative is to accept conflict and struggle as unavoidable.

The journey involves groping and muddling through. The cross and resurrection of Christ are indeed paradigms for Christian life, but they are not magic keys by which to "decipher political and economic problems."[32]

Unquestionably, Boff's Christology serves a given public human need. His is a clear case of soteriology shaping Christology. He is undeterred by theologians like Pannenberg who anxiously guard against projecting human needs onto a picture of Christ. But Boff unabashedly asserts that "the real question is who, or what cause, is served by a given christology."[33] He is suspicious of those who think otherwise and whose enlightened Christologies often turn out to be a cover for conservative political positions and in fact "serve to reinforce the status quo." He is also suspicious of theologians in affluent circumstances who adopt a liberation approach but never really analyze the social conditions of oppression and, failing that, silently support oppression.[34]

Of course, theologians like Boff and Sobrino are not indifferent to the classic question of the *person* of Jesus (in whom there is the unity of the two natures, etc.), but they are wary lest by moving too quickly to such questions they fall into the error of constructing Christologies which thwart rather than enhance the liberating *work* of Christ.[35] Boff, for example, does not merely assume the divinity of Christ but approaches that question from the view of Jesus' unsurpassable humanity. For him, presuppositions about divinity should not determine what sort of humanity can be found in Jesus. What is striking about Jesus is *not* that Jesus is divine in some self-evident way, but that he is so utterly human. Therefore, what one must account for is not the supposedly divine qualities which set Jesus apart *from* humanity, but those qualities which identify Jesus so intimately *with* humanity. All humans are essentially "Christic," independently of any encounter with Jesus; they are "at heart" expectant, eagerly waiting for liberation. Human beings, then, are inherently capable of the divine and look for the divine and so, says Boff, when Jesus comes as Liberator, their innate human capacity, their longing, is fulfilled in the genuine humanity of Jesus as Liberator. Even when presented in this condensed form it is clear why his Christological reflections begin with the note, "Only God could be as human as Jesus."[36]

Jon Sobrino, who teaches philosophy and theology in El Salvador, is in total agreement with Boff about approaching the question of the divinity of Jesus from the perspective of his humanity. Like Boff, he does not question that the formula of Chalcedon, as an ultimate statement about the personal unity of Jesus with God, must be maintained as historically necessary and fundamental. The problem is how to interpret it, or how to assess its place and function. Sobrino regards dogma as but one of several expressions of faith (along with gospel or proclamation, and with catechesis or teaching). Dogma was never intended to exhaust the meaning of faith in Jesus but to protect the faith from misunderstanding. Just as dogma sets out certain limits on what faith cannot mean, dogma also has its own limits and must be interpreted in order that the *intention* of the dogma be properly understood. Authoritative formulas reflect the history of the time in which they were written. For the sake of their originally intended meaning they, too, must be translated into terms appropriate for successive generations. In that sense dogmas are like Scripture. How one approaches them is crucial.

Sobrino agrees also that dogmatic statements about the divinity of Jesus cannot be approached head-on. "Jesus' divinity is not self-evident, and the dogmatic formula does not make it so. We can profess that Jesus is the eternal Son of the Father, but only indirectly on the basis of historical happenings . . . (e.g. his preaching, his activity and his death) and on the basis of the eschatological happening of his resurrection."[37] Thus the indirect approach begins with the history of Jesus and later arrives at dogma as the ultimate conclusion of faith based on the historical witness. Dogma is not the premise with which one begins in order to prove something, Sobrino claims, but should be regarded as hymns of praise, or as doxological responses to the New Testament in which "Jesus' distinctiveness and uniqueness show up first and foremost in his distinct and unique relationship with the one he calls his Father."[38]

Thus the christology elaborated here maintains the dogmatic statements, but it offers a different approach. . . . Instead of beginning with the doxological affirmations of the incarnation of the eternal Son in Jesus of Nazareth (the theology of *descent*), it ends up with the doxological statement that this Jesus of Nazareth is the eternal Son. . . . The advantage of my approach here over that of the traditional christology of descent is that it regards the history of Jesus as basic and essential to the dogmatic assertion that Christ is the eternal Son.[39]

Sobrino and other liberation theologians, while they do not begin with the orthodox creeds, eventually do end up there. They begin with the question of praxis—how to serve the needs of the oppressed. Their reflection on this question guides their interpretation of the life, ministry, death, and resurrection of Jesus, who emerges from that reading as Jesus the Liberator. What is different is not that their interpretation of Jesus is any less than what the dogmatic statements of the church have professed Jesus to be (for example, truly human, truly divine) but that salvation as liberation of the oppressed is now authorized as the will of God and as a sign of the kingdom of God on earth. God's kingdom initiated in Jesus means that "preference for the poor" is more than a left-wing political bias. Indeed, if Jesus the Liberator is also God, then liberation is the mandate of God and those who are Christian have no alternative than to discover in what ways they—as followers of Jesus—can show their solidarity with the oppressed people of the earth.

Liberation theologians may indeed end with the orthodox creed of classical Christianity, but their way of beginning with the historical Jesus as Liberator means that they end with a distinctive view of Jesus as Savior. The Christology of liberationist theologians is by their own account orthodox, but its public and political implications—one might say its soteriological implications—are nonetheless radical. The salvation wrought by God in Jesus is a divine mandate for Christian action in the arena of political change.

Salvation and Human Experience

In my view [the] gulf between *faith* and *experience* is one of the fundamental reasons for the present-day crisis among Christians . . .[40]

Father Edward Schillebeeckx, like theologians of liberation, is concerned to bring faith in Christ into the public domain, but he emphasizes common human experience rather than history. "God acts in history" has become a commonplace theological expression even though those who so write and speak would differ widely on how to interpret the meaning of the sentence. The reigning consensus—that salvation is not an utterly spiritual, individualistic, or private occurrence nor an event which is totally remote from ordinary history—means that God's saving acts must somehow occur within or coincide with public history. In the opinion of some, then, salvation is a hidden dimension or feature of secular history. For others, history is too full of disaster to make a simple equation of history and salvation, but history, nevertheless, is the place where people must make decisions about either the eventual destruction of humanity or the salvation of humanity.

Others would stress the fact that the partiality of every particular view of history makes all historical judgments so relative that only if one knew the outcome, the end, of history could its unity and meaning be known. The fact that all viewpoints are relative argues for an eschatological view of salvation; thus Jesus can be Savior only if as an apocalyptic figure he reveals what the whole sweep of history will be at the End, regardless of how ambiguous or disastrous history is until then.

What is common in all these proposals is the presumption that salvation must somehow be connected with history, lest salvation lose its meaning and truthfulness. Following the Enlightenment, the most damaging assault on the credibility of Christian claims for Jesus came from the historical scholars who, by relativizing every historical event and viewpoint, undermined the authority of both Scripture and the church. It became clear that additional appeals to history would never rescue Christianity from the relativity of its historical status as merely one religion among many. Nothing about its historical origins is itself immune from historical contingencies; even the revealed propositions of Christianity are no less historically relative, no matter how vehemently theologians assert their status as revelation.

Edward Schillebeeckx[41] accepts the consensus that God acts in ordinary history, but he virtually abandons all such efforts to establish the meaning of salvation by means of a theory of history. His massive two-volume Christology (a third is projected) is in large part predicated on a shift away from history as the major correlate to which theology must give an account. In Schillebeeckx's Christology, the authority of history has shifted toward the authority of experience. Schillebeeckx doubts that most thoughtful people are troubled by the challenges of history, even when they are fully aware of the import of historical relativity upon all truth claims, whether religious or scientific. Somehow a person can go on living as a Christian, as a Westerner, as a middle-class professional even when one is completely conscious of the relativity, partiality, and contingency of one's circumstances. Historical relativity—in itself—need not shake a person's belief in the truthfulness or meaning of Christianity any more than political corruption in itself destroys one's belief that democratic government is superior to rule by tyrants.

The historical relativity of Christianity (which seemed to undermine its significance or truthfulness for previous generations) is therefore not the problem Schillebeeckx addresses. For him, faith forfeits its claim to meaning or truthfulness when it loses any connection with human experience. The truly critical situation, for Schillebeeckx, is when the basis of experience is itself removed and when

> people are no longer clear why salvation should be sought specifically in this Jesus of two thousand years ago. In that case there is no longer any experience of salvation in Jesus. And in the end faith is undermined if it has to look for salvation from someone on the authority of others, if there is nothing that corresponds to it in the whole of their personal experience. Faith then quietly vanishes from life, dying through its own irrelevance and a short circuit of human experience.[42]

Because Schillebeeckx, a very influential Roman Catholic theologian, has been so forthright in emphasizing the importance of relating the claims of faith to human experience, he has been vulnerable to criticism from several quarters. The Vatican curia has challenged him on the question whether this emphasis undermines the teaching authority of the Church of Rome, and he has been required to reaffirm his loyalty to that tradition. Protestant theologians like John Macquarrie have placed him in the liberal tradition of Schleiermacher, in particular asking whether it is the New Testament witness or the "experience of salvation" which ultimately controls Schillebeeckx's interpretation of Christ.[43] But even his critics are obliged to acknowledge that no other systematic theologian has shown himself to be as knowledgeable of New Testament scholarship as Father Schillebeeckx.

In his earlier work, *Christ: The Sacrament of the Encounter with God,* Schillebeeckx had approached Christology in the more traditional manner of beginning with the historical doctrines and then, somewhat deductively, showing the implications of Christological dogma for Christian faith and life today.[44] In contrast, his two large "Jesus" books represent his determination to base a contemporary interpretation of Jesus on two different foundations: modern exegetical studies of the New Testament and an experiential concept of salvation.[45] Like the liberation theologians, Schillebeeckx assumes that God's definitive salvation comes through Jesus Christ; he is convinced, however, that this truth can itself be lost if not properly grounded in historical-critical exegesis of the Bible and in an intelligible view of salvation, while arguing further that no view of salvation is intelligible if it is not in some sense experiential.

> Salvation is an experiential concept, and therefore it must reflect at least partially what man *experiences* as "saving". The experience of salvation as saving is part of the concept of salvation. That does not mean that salvation is "everywhere and fully and completely a reality of experience" but it must at least "partially and at least sometimes" be experienced specifically by those affected as saving.[46]

And so, the concept of salvation must be grounded—at least in part—on experience. It is at this point that confessional, neoorthodox theologians are likely to get nervous, fearing that the objective truth of God's revelation in Christ as the Word will be judged according to the merely human and subjective standards of "feelings" and personal religious emotions. Of course, that very fear often reflects the prior assumption that "experience" can refer only to the sense experience or feelings of human subjects.

Schillebeeckx argues that the subjectivist and sensationalist view of experience is too limited, and is usually tied to the dualism of Cartesian philosophy. He thinks that "we have grown away from the Cartesian dualism of subjectivity and objectivity," and that theologians as well should give it up and get beyond merely scoffing at "experience" as if it can refer only to subjective feeling. Experience is a dialectical interplay between perception and thought (or interpretation). Thus, "on the one hand thought makes experience possible, while on the other hand it is experience that makes new thinking necessary."

> Therefore "to find salvation in Jesus" is not *either* a subjective experience *or* an objective fact. To experience salvation is experience and interpretation at the same time. In experiencing we identify what is experienced, and we do this by classifying what we experience in terms of already known models and concepts, patterns or categories. . . . Consequently experience is a richly nuanced totality in which

experience, thought and interpretation run together in the same way as past, present and expectations of the future.[47]

In other words, Schillebeeckx regrets that so many theologians assume that experience is the total contrast or antithesis of revelation, of faith, of divine truth and genuine salvation. Revelation, like salvation, he insists, always occurs in human experiences, not apart from human experience, "but at the same time it summons us from what we take for granted in our limited world. It is therefore not to be found in any direct appeal to our so-called self-evident experiences within the world."[48]

By accepting both the authority of the New Testament and the authority of experience as points of reference for his salvation Christology, Schillebeeckx has shown that he thinks one can be both Christian and contemporary but—to say the least—even these brief comments on experience are sufficient warning that Schillebeeckx's proposal is not as clear and crisp as those theologies which trade on sharp disjunctions between revelation and experience, or between salvation as objective atonement and the subjective experience of being saved. He regards such disjunctions as abstractions from the totality of experience from which all language and definitions emerge. It is impossible, he says, to begin with the abstract notion of revelation and only then relate it to experience; such a move goes against the very "structure of revelation" which is rooted in experience. To contrast the two is a false dilemma because "one does not work without the other. *Revelation* is brought about through *experiences*."[49] This certainly does not mean that Schillebeeckx collapses revelation into any and all notions of experience; for him there is an important distinction, albeit a very subtle one, between revelation *in* experience and revelation *as* experiences.

So for believers, *revelation* is an *action of God* as *experienced* by believers and *interpreted* in religious language and therefore expressed in human terms, in the dimension of our utterly human history. The all-pervasive, authoritative element of revelation in this complex context is not this interpretative experience itself but what can be experienced in it. . . . *In* our human experiences we can *experience* something that transcends our experience and proclaims itself in that experience as unexpected grace.[50]

Robert Schreiter observes that, for Schillebeeckx, experience has something of a sacred character which no single set of concepts—religious, philosophical, or scientific—can fully grasp. Because no language is fully adequate to experience, it requires a plurality of approaches.[51] Even theology is not exempt from all of the problems associated with understanding reality as it is experienced. Whether in theology or science, every articulation of experience will be conditioned by the experiencer's tradition of models, theories, or doctrines of faith, just as every one of these must be open to challenge by new experiences. It is unhelpful merely to assert that either experience or doctrine is the final authority. The long debate on this matter at least seems to have demonstrated the even more subtle point that whether one speaks of scientific theories or of the doctrines of faith, they are never *simply* and *directly* derived from experience, however otherwise dependent they are on experience for confirmation or illumination. Theories are hypotheses, envisionments, human creations, or inventions—and not mere summations of accumulated data. So, too, doctrine: "Expressions of faith are . . . also theoretical expressions and not simply expressions of experience." For Schillebeeckx this means that every doctrine or expression of faith must be open to reconsideration in light of new experiences (influenced as *they* are, of course, by new interpretive theories), even as all experiences in turn must be tested by the faith which the process of revelation sustains.[52]

In Schillebeeckx's view, both revelation and salvation are *initiated* by God as well as grounded in experience. But how are revelation and salvation related to each other? He argues that salvation has a certain priority. Writing in response to questioners, he first reiterates the continuity between revelation and experience.

> I wrote the two books about Jesus in the light of the conviction, taken for granted in both Old and New Testaments, that revelation and experience are not opposites. . . . There is no revelation without experience. God's revelation is the opposite of our achievements or plans, but . . . this in no way excludes the fact that revelation also includes human plans and experiences and thus in no way suggests that revelation should fall outside our experience.[53]

He then calls attention to the fact that for those first disciples who encountered Jesus during his life and after his resurrection, the encounter "gave their own lives new meaning and significance. . . .

This change in the direction of their lives was the result of their real encounter with Jesus . . . [and] was not something over which they had taken the initiative." The experience of salvation was primary, but that experience then provoked the following question:

"Who is the one who is able to do these things?" In other words the New Testament speaks of the person of Jesus in such a way as to clarify how Jesus was able to do what he did. It is not the faith of the disciples which makes Jesus God's decisive revelation, although they could not have said anything about revelation without such an experience of faith; the experience is an essential part of the concept of revelation. . . . *Soteriology is the way to christology*—that is clear enough from the New Testament.[54]

By now that last sentence is a familiar theme to the reader; and it leads to the implied question about lostness.

The Constants of Being Human

Although salvation as an experiential term is fundamental to understanding Schillebeeckx's Christology, he has no single term as the equivalent for the condition of lostness from which people can experience being saved, and there is no direct route to uncover what lostness would refer to in his soteriologically based Christology. A slight detour is necessary here in order to explore what "human" means as a critical clue for grasping Schillebeeckx's concept of salvation.

By enlarging the meaning of experience beyond the merely "subjective" on the one hand or the merely "objective" on the other hand, Schillebeeckx has also opened the possibility for expanding what salvation can mean. In a late chapter of the second of the two Jesus books, "The Height and Breadth and Depth of Human Salvation," he proposes an anthropological basis for a view of salvation that goes beyond the simple choice between conventional "subjective" and "objective" views. His proposal is made in light of the modern critical awareness that every definition of human nature is inevitably partial and thus faulty. Some have even led to totalitarianism. For him, therefore, the widespread "critical awareness" of educated people today is a very positive factor, because it fosters a healthy suspicion of all definitions of humankind, even of those put forward by Christians. And so what he offers is in no way a proposed final blueprint for humanity. "Our time has become more modest here. Nature, 'ordinances of creation' and Evolution (with a capital E) cannot give us any criteria for what is livable and true, good and happy humanity, and thus for what makes up . . . ethically responsible action which furthers this true humanity."[55] Modern reason is critical, not dogmatic, suspicious of all preexisting definitions of humankind, not committed to any one view at the expense of all others. Nevertheless, some kind of general definition of humankind is necessary if there is to be any basis for shared conversation about those criteria which can best serve to guide humans in acting together for the sake of humanity.

Human salvation is at the center of Schillebeeckx's interest here, but he is very nontraditional in his approach. He, too, exhibits that severely critical awareness—characteristic of our time—which makes him suspicious of all salvation schemes. Even religious ones are suspect, inasmuch as they often conceal or even support narrow political and economic interests. They can lead to human oppression rather than salvation. Although he offers no perfect or finished definition of human worth—that is not possible—he nevertheless wishes to look for those "constitutive aspects" of human nature which must be taken into account by every effort to establish "specific norms for a better assessment of human worth and thus for human *salvation.*" Those constitutive aspects are in every case relational characteristics; in other words, regardless of particular historical and cultural circumstances, there are certain relational structures which are always constitutive of humanity.[56] In a section called "The system of co-ordinates of man and his salvation" he describes what he calls the "anthropological constants" which are characteristic of all human beings. None of the constants is of itself a "value." Each of them, however, does open up or point to a certain structure or type of relationship without which humans could not exist. To state it more simply still, each of these constants is a way of saying, "Take heed, here in this relation apart from which no person can be truly human, the worth of humanity will either be enhanced or threatened." Hence the seven anthropological constants are relational spheres wherein the essential *values* affecting human salvation are to be found, and where the norms for genuine well-being or

salvation have to be worked out. In each of the following coordi-
nates, which constitute humanity, the question of human salvation
is at stake. They can be listed briefly.

First is the relationship of humankind to the wider sphere of nature, which includes one's relation to one's own body as well as to
the ecological environment.

> If Christian *salvation* is in fact the *salvation of men*, it will also have
> essential connections with this first "anthropological constant". . . .
> Christian salvation is also connected with ecology and the conditions
> and burdens which . . . life here and now lays on men. [To claim
> otherwise] . . . is to dream of a salvation for *angels,* but not for *men.*

This does not mean that humans would be better off in a purely
natural world—in fact, they could not survive in such a world—but
it does imply that they must use their culture's technology and "in-
strumental reason" to sustain the sort of cultural environment which
will emancipate humans from the natural environment without destroying the ecological basis on which all cultures must depend.[57]

The second constant is that all persons are destined for relationships with other persons. "The co-humanity with which we encounter one another as people . . . is an anthropological constant
which looks for norms without which whole or livable humanity is
impossible." Society is more than the I-thou relationship. For the
fullness of humanness, it takes more than a "thou" and an "I"; to
make a society there must be "she," "he," and "they," besides
"thee" and "me."[58]

The third essential dimension or constant (often dismissed as
something that is disposable) is institutional or social structure.
Schillebeeckx insists that here is indeed an *essential* dimension.
Institutions are sometimes regarded as independent of human action
("You can't fight city hall") or even *de*-humanizing, but institutional
structures are a constant which "shows a sphere of values" where
human beings can shape institutions so that they do not enslave and
debase people but liberate them and give them protection.[59]

The fourth constant is that all persons are conditioned by their
historical and geographical situation; it is not possible to detach
oneself from time and space. The task of value clarification here is
the critical hermeneutical one, namely, how to interpret our own
tradition with all its historical limits in order to reappropriate it

without the dangerous presumption that our local standpoint is above history or is unlimited. This danger has been obvious in some interpretations of the Bible, of course, but also seems especially evident among Western nations which think that their claim on prosperity is an absolute which exempts them from human limitation and from international solidarity toward the poor nations of the world.[60]

The fifth constant is the relation between theory and practice without which humanity would not be able to adapt to the changing circumstances which come upon every culture. The stability and survival, indeed the salvation of human beings, depends not on "will and thought" alone or on "the power of the strongest" but on the "only humanly responsible guarantee of a permanent culture which is increasingly worthy of man," namely, a combination of theory and practice.

No view of salvation is complete if it neglects the sixth anthropological constant, a constant believers in God would call religion, but one that is found in any culture whatsoever and which might also be called the utopian element. Human beings construct

> views of life, views of society, world-views and general theories of life in which [they] express what ultimately inspires them, what humanity they choose in the last resort, what they really live for and what makes life worth living. [Whatever form this view takes] . . . it is always a form of faith . . . which cannot be scientifically investigated, or . . . completely rationalized.

Faith—understood in the more general sense which includes religious faith—is, in this scheme, constitutive of what gives value, worthwhileness, and wholeness to humanity; therefore, any proposal for human salvation must include this anthropological constant as well.[61]

Schillebeeckx believes that the constants thus far described must finally be *synthesized* because they are characteristic of human culture which is, in fact, "an irreducible autonomous reality" and thus cannot be reduced to any of its constants—either to the sphere of the seemingly "spiritual" values or to the sphere of physical and social sciences—without disturbing the whole. The synthesis itself is the seventh constant. "The reality which heals men and brings them salvation lies in this synthesis. . . ."[62] Any view of salvation which focuses exclusively on religion and spirit or on political liberation is simply not adequate either to the scriptural vision of salvation or to the essential dimensions of what it means to be human.

Schillebeeckx believes that the biblical view of salvation is grounded in human experience and that the seven anthropological constants offer a way of explicating, in contemporary critical language, the experiential character of "the height and breadth and depth of human salvation." He accepts the plurality of views about what human nature is, and acknowledges that "the pain of this pluralism is part of our *condition humaine*," but for the sake of human salvation we must cope with it and find ways to coordinate the many dimensions of being human. His dual approach—based on *both* Scripture and experience—is not contradictory.

> Christian salvation, in the . . . biblical tradition called redemption and meant as salvation from God *for men,* is concerned with the whole system of co-ordinates in which man can really be man. This salvation—the wholeness of man—cannot be sought [exclusively] in one or other of these constants . . . . On the other hand, the synthesis of all this is clearly an "already now" and a "not yet". . . .[63]

Lostness as Isolation: Salvation as Reconciliation

Inasmuch as wholeness of life, that is, life as God intends life to be, depends upon coordination, cooperation, synthesis, integration, and harmonious relatedness among all the creatures, we need not search far for the implied meaning of lostness. It is not hard to define, and it is evident in all the structures of life-as-experienced. No one can live fully when isolated, disowned, remote, discounted, or outcast. The forms of lostness can be readily listed by following Schillebeeckx's summary of the constants of being human. To be lost is—

- to be cut off from, or to endanger, the environment upon which all life depends;
- to feel alienated from one's own body;
- to be denied or to resist all interaction with others whether through writing, reading, or conversation;
- to be caught in social structures which isolate people according to class or race or beliefs or sex;

● to interpret one's own tradition, one's own time and place, as the absolute and exclusive measure of human meaning and truth, or to be excluded by those who do;

● to reject all criticism of favorite theories or to refuse a different practice when suggested by new theories, or a different theory suggested by a new praxis, and thus to refuse to adapt to new demands;

● to exist without purpose, vision, ideals, goals, or to regard these as useless, as not essential for life or worth arguing, thinking, and caring about;

● to neglect the plurality of life's dimensions, or to be subjected to a repressive system that is "reductionistic."

This is one small sample of how "lostness" can be described as the disturbance of those fundamental relationships without which human life is less than whole.

When one considers Schillebeeckx's Christological enterprise in the perspective of his critical anthropology, then it is clear that *both* his reading of the Jesus story in the New Testament witness *and* his reading of the human situation influence each other. This is exactly his intention, and, contrary to critics for whom the New Testament should primarily control the interpretation of Jesus or to those who think that "a living modern theology must begin from men's present-day experiences,"[64] Schillebeeckx goes to great length (indeed!) to show how *both* must be stressed. To insist on *either* the authority of the New Testament as primary *or* the authority of contemporary experience as primary is simply a false dilemma. In our critical time, it is simply impossible to begin with the New Testament and then "apply" it to the human situation, because every interpreter is already influenced by the situation. He writes, "My approach in the two books about Jesus has been to see . . . the actual situation in which we live today as an intrinsic and determinative element for understanding God's revelation in the history of Israel and of Jesus which Christians have experienced as salvation from God for men and women. . . ."[65] Thus, Schillebeeckx's anthropology does clearly determine his interpretation of Jesus as Savior, not exclusively or primarily but in a method which has been called a "mutually critical correlation." In Schillebeeckx's case that simply means that his read-ing of how Jesus is experienced as God's proffer of salvation in the New Testament is a critical guide for understanding the experience of salvation today, while the experiential character of salvation to-day—illumined by the dimensions of lostness uncovered by the "anthropological constants"—is a critical guide for reading the New Testament.

It has been sufficiently emphasized that Schillebeeckx, because of his complex view of experience, does not hesitate to insist that experience, critically interpreted, is one of two sources which de-termine what God's salvation in Jesus can mean today. This becomes especially evident in the first of the two Jesus books, in which he deals primarily with the New Testament Gospels. He does not dwell very long on the question of the historical Jesus which, although it is a basic issue, should not become a "positivistic obsession."[66] What does occupy Schillebeeckx in his extensive review of the exegetical literature is the Gospels' presentation of Jesus as he was experienced. No figure can be called historical independently of his or her social interactions; indeed a person "forms the focus of an extensive area."

By redefining "person" in more social terms, Schillebeeckx can then assert that what "counts" *for* a person's "historicity" is not narrow "facts" allegedly established without any social or personal bias. The historicality of Jesus is found, not by dismissing biased accounts of his effect on people, but precisely by noting his influence and interactions as reported in the Gospels. The "historical starting point" then is not Jesus of Nazareth in total isolation from the relativities of his humanity. Schillebeeckx's definition of human as relatedness would imply that an abstract Jesus of Nazareth would be nonhuman. Nor is the starting point the kerygma or message as a literary deposit abstracted from all historical relativity. Because every historian who asks who Jesus is would have to deal with "the actual effect of the man," notably with "the concrete experiences of the first local communities of Christians," the ultimate *historical* basis for Christology is "the movement which Jesus himself started in the first century."[67]

Historical relativity abounds in the New Testament, but it does not preclude a genuine unity or a constancy in the New Testament.

"The unitive factor" is the Christian movement itself. In other words, it is

> a Christian oneness of experience which does indeed take its unity from its pointing to the one figure of Jesus, while nonetheless pluriform in its verbal expression. . . . The constant factor here is that particular groups of people find final salvation imparted by God in Jesus of Nazareth.[68]

The New Testament is the literary deposit of a movement centering in Jesus, but the singular importance of Jesus is not overshadowed thereby. "No Christianity without Jesus but equally none without Christians," whose "congregation-based experiences deposited in Scripture are the constant factor," while the New Testament's several Christologies are the variable responses to that unitive factor.

Schillebeeckx believes that people experienced Jesus as good news, as Savior come from God, even before Jesus was crucified, and that if there had been no public movement, if no one had so experienced Jesus, there would have been no crucifixion. One must *first* account for the crucifixion in terms of the influence Jesus had on those who were drawn to him, and only *then* account for what must have happened that the Jesus who came teaching and preaching became, after the crucifixion, the Christ who was preached. There would have been no movement without Jesus, but without the movement it strains one's historical credulity to think that certain civil and religious authorities would have sought to crucify a teacher who attracted no attention.[69]

Our discussion to this point has stressed how Schillebeeckx's description of the human constants guides his exposition of the gospel writings. We can summarize: The foundation of the Gospels is the *disciples' experience of Jesus as the locus wherein God has revealed himself as salvation of and for humanity in definitive fashion.*[70] The miracle stories, the parables, the activity of Jesus, and the various designations of Jesus as "Lord," "Son of David," "prophet," and the like, all reflect that experience. Beginning with the Q community, what is so striking about Jesus is not simply the miraculous, but the *source* of all his activity. In this tradition Jesus himself is saying, "If it is by the finger of God that I cast out demons, then the kingdom of God has come upon you" (Luke 11:20).

The driving out of demons and healing of the sick point in Jesus to the "time of salvation" in the latter days, a time now dawning. God himself is now active in Jesus ("with the finger of God", that is, in Semitic idiom, "by God's intervention", Ex. 8:10; Dan. 9:10). . . . The Q community is thereby able to present not so much a christology as a soteriology: salvation in Jesus, imparted by God.[71]

Schillebeeckx reads the Gospels as soteriology. Instead of looking for confirmation of dogmatic Christological definitions of Jesus' identity, he notices, for instance in Mark's gospel, how Jesus is not worried about his identity but

in all that he does, his identity is to identify himself with people in distress in order to release them from their self-estrangement and restore them to themselves, so that they are made free again for others and for God. . . . At any rate, in Jesus salvation, a final good, has been encountered as a matter of personal experience. That a divine mystery lies hidden here is for the time being passed over in silence."[72]

Again and again Schillebeeckx stresses that in Jesus' life God is experienced as the One who is open to sinners and that in the presence of Jesus it is not possible to fast because of the joy of salvation experienced there. Much is made also of the experience of table fellowship, where Jesus shows how God reaches beyond social and religious conventions to invite the outcasts, the separated, the disowned, and the rejected, including them in the scope of God's rule.

When Jesus restores outcasts to joyful relationship with God and frees them to and for wholeness, he himself epitomizes God's way of ruling in the world and God's way of salvation. The connections between salvation thus revealed in Jesus and salvation today are made by interpreting salvation in terms of the full range of relationships that are essential for being human. That which heals, in other words, the salvation which Jesus epitomizes, is found *within* the synthesis of the here-and-now relationships which are necessary for wholeness of life.

Chapter Five

THE SAVIOR AS
TOTAL PRESENCE AND
AS MEDIATOR OF GOD

I do not share a widespread assumption that the churches are irrelevant. On the contrary, . . . the churches and the quasi-independent evangelists are teaching up a storm, and people are getting the messages. The results, for the most part, are very unethical. They amount to what Dorothee Soelle has called "christofascism."[1]

On the dedication page of the book quoted above, the author, Tom F. Driver, has written,

> To all who have suffered at the hands of people
> who claimed to act in the name of Christ,
> this book is dedicated.

The charge has frequently been made that Christology in practice encourages Christians to be arrogant or cruel toward others in the name of Jesus. One of the most radical responses to that charge comes from Tom Driver, who insists that the measure by which to evaluate every theological doctrine should be its "socioethical" consequence and who then applies this test especially to traditional Christology. He is appalled by the unethical use of Christology. "The attempt of Christians to hide their conscience behind Jesus, making him responsible for their decisions and looking to him to forgive moral failure, does not fool the world."[2]

Christians must learn to *think* differently about Jesus; one of the principal detectors for locating faulty thinking about Jesus (that is, Christological error) is its ethical consequences. The fruits, and not the roots, are what concern Driver, who therefore fully agrees with Rosemary Ruether's book on Christian anti-Semitism, *Faith and Fratricide*. It is the impact of Christology upon the ethics of Christianity toward Jews and Judaism which convinces Ruether that traditional Christology must be changed, because "any doctrine which reduces one's ethical sensibility must have something wrong with it."[3]

The "something wrong" with most Christologies, in Driver's view, is the notion that Christ is the center, model, or norm, or that Christ is somehow absolute or final. Thus, Driver is critical of thinking of Jesus Christ as the

- center of creation, because this can too easily be taken to mean that even government hierarchies, as well as the starry heavens, are divinely established;
- center of humanity, which tends to fix eternally the definition of being human;
- center of history, which can be taken to imply that there can be nothing fundamentally new;
- center of society, which has encouraged a domineering church to impose its Christian standards on all social structures.

Christians should simply give up the claim that Christ is the center, for two reasons. First, "to think historically, in the modern sense, is to give up centers and abiding norms. It is to enter wholeheartedly upon the seas of relativity, where all things change . . . [and] no historical event may claim to be central to all others." Historical thinking, by definition, precludes a fixed center. Second, biblical scholarship has shown that the scriptural and eschatological mode of thinking itself is closer to historical thinking than to the more classical notion of fixed, eternal, and unchanging centers, norms, or definitions of truth. The Christ of Scripture comes as the eschatological future, as promise, and not as the fixed norm. To be faithful to Jesus "one must refuse him as model or central norm.

He himself seems not to have needed a center of history. What he relied on was the power of a loving God."[4] But when Christ is thought of as the center or as the final, once-for-all-Lord, then believers will always be looking backward to the past instead of looking foward, trusting in Christ's own promise that he is not to be found in past images but on the leading edge of history. One can find Christ only by pressing forward to God's promised future as one lives fully in the present.

When Christians think of Christ as the fixed center or norm, they then adopt a concept of Christ as the measure or norm of Christian life, and neglect the question whether their deeds have liberated and served the neighbor. Instead of honoring the neighbor who shares the "present-future" with them, Christians are preoccupied with the a fixed concept of Christ oriented to the past. Driver argues that such nonhistorical and nonbiblical Christologies are at the base of Christians' unethical treatment of others, and that the Christ who is known through such Christologies must be given up for the Christ of faith. "The Christ of faith is not the one we knew yesterday but the one we expect to meet while going forward."[5]

Driver's interpretation, of course, is somewhat parallel to liberation theologians' insistence that theology attend to the first step of serving the neighbor; but, as we have already observed, most liberation theologians conclude with fairly orthodox Christologies. What distinguishes Driver's proposal for a socioethically responsible Christology is his more radical attack on all ideas or definitions of Christ as final, as norm, as center. Such ideas, Driver believes, are unthinkable for the historical consciousness of modern persons. In addition, they are not consistent with the New Testament Christ who is "Christ future." Finally, such notions imply an exclusivity and "absoluteness" which remove Christ totally from reality as interpreted today. An absolutely exclusive Christ would not be human, because such a Christ would be immune from cultural influences. A Christ who is not *relative* makes no sense "in the Einsteinian universe, which has *no center* and in which every structure is a dynamic relationality of *moving* components."[6] In the view of Driver, then, the source of the unethical practices of Christians is unethical Christology, that is, thinking that is wrong because it ascribes to Christ such categories as finality, absoluteness, centrality, and norm. "We are in danger of losing Christ utterly through our attempts to make [Christ] a fixed and eternal point for all time."[7]

Obviously, Driver is willing to abandon some of the terms by which theology has traditionally made claims for the significance of Christ, claims which have been important elements of Christian belief for centuries. He believes that his proposal is not only consistent with faith in Christ but also is supported by Scripture, especially by the eschatological, future-oriented reading of the New Testament favored by modern biblical scholars. Furthermore, it fits the historical awareness of contemporary people for whom to believe in a Christ who is nonhistorical, nonrelative, abstracted from culture, and whose significance or truth is once and for all fixed is to believe in the unbelievable, because such a Christ is neither real nor human. Like so many present-day theologians, Driver is responding to the challenge of historical consciousness which not only undermines the absolute claims of traditional Christology but also exposes the unethical uses of those doctrines in the history of the church. His objection to classical Christology is that when believers give central place to Christ, they inevitably assume an attitude of arrogant superiority toward non-Christians. Christology thus reduces ethical sensitivity.

Yet not all radical or liberal theologians are as ready to reject Christian claims for the uniqueness and finality of Jesus. An equally "radical" theologian, Thomas J. J. Altizer, has recently argued that Christianity—and *Christianity alone*—knows a Word, indeed a total Word, which is not only the antithesis of all human words but is that Word which alone brings the kingdom of God. When Altizer published *The Gospel of Christian Atheism,* he was dismissed by many mainline theologians. His recent book on Jesus should earn him a new hearing, at least for the absolute uniqueness of Jesus as the Word who alone can save humankind from the destructive perils of modernity.[8] Altizer acknowledges that "historical consciousness," which theologians take for granted as the inescapable condition of intellectual life today, permeates all interpretations of Jesus. All speech, all thought, all proposals about Jesus' significance, all language that has been or ever will be spoken about Jesus, is relative. The "absolute" of such "historicism" is that there is no absolute. What, then, could possibly be the antithesis of the relativity of all language about Jesus? Altizer's response: the language *of* Jesus.

When the language *of* Jesus is truly encountered, it cannot be simply categorized, explained, or understood; in short it cannot be relativized. Historical consciousness may indeed relativize all language about Jesus but the *language of Jesus* relativizes all language as such; it even relativizes historical relativity.

Lostness as False Consciousness

As noted earlier, Driver would urge believers "to enter wholeheartedly upon the seas of relativity" with confidence that as they immerse themselves in the ebb and flow of history Christ will be there in every moment. Relativity is the permeating condition of every reality. Nothing that is real, not even the reality of Christ, is exempt. In this age of relativity, believers should not hark back to past definitions of Christ in order to find in them a fixed rock upon which the church can anchor itself as a wedge against change. "A Christianity captive to Christ past will be increasingly forced to draw lines of resistance to new forms of human encounter. . . ."[9] Driver is optimistic that, once old Christologies are repudiated, Jesus as Savior will foster the development of those new forms of being human which are now emerging.

Contrary to Driver's optimism about relativity, Altizer quite pointedly asks whether the seas of relativity are all that promising for humanity's voyage into the future. Awareness of historical relativity itself has a history, as anyone blessed (or cursed) with historical consciousness would readily admit. That I was born into circumstances in which I was taught to think historically is as much a matter of historical accident as my being born into a Christian family and being taught the Bible and not the Koran. Confronting the "accident" of one's life situation and the relativity of one's own tradition and one's own beliefs is a well-known experience to college freshmen, or to villagers with transistor radios anywhere on the globe. But such consciousness does not avert freshmen from even greater zeal for nonhistorical fundamentalism nor does it keep villagers from uncritical loyalty to nationalistic leaders or clergy from uncritical denominationalism.

Historical awareness can strip away every pretense of absolute authority, it can see through every camouflage of certainty, and it can doubt all claims for a "truth" that is beyond doubt. Everyone, once bitten by the bug of historical consciousness, is forever immune, forever "delivered" from the naive belief that one's village, family, religion, or culture is at the center of history or the universe, and thus historical consciousness does deliver us from false certainty. But, as the people of Israel learned, deliverance from captivity can also be experienced as being thrown into the wilderness, just as the sea of relativity can be experienced as the threat of drowning. When drowning in relativity one naturally reaches for help and does not reject it even though the only help available is also awash in relativity. Indeed, one understandably clings all the more fervently.

Only in the modern period of historical and global awareness have absolutist religious and political systems taken on such ferocity. Both religious fundamentalism and political totalitarianism derive much of their power from the refusal of their adherents to yield to the nagging and fear-filled suspicion that what they blindly cling to is also mere flotsam and jetsam on the sea of history. They desperately need to suppress that suspicion because to admit it to awareness— to accept what historical awareness presses upon them—would be to admit that they are not really being "saved" because their flotation device is no more absolute than they who cling to it, for it too is doomed.

It is because relativity—born of historical consciousness—provokes human beings into reaching so desperately for absolutistic forms of religious and political authority, that Altizer—the so-called radical theologian—cannot be optimistic about embracing relativity. In the nuclear age, humanity is all the more threatened by human madness provoked by fear. So long as people live with historical consciousness there can be no end to this threat, because so long as people are made anxious by their awareness of their own relativity, humanity can never rest easy that the world is rid of potential tyrants preying on the anxieties of the masses. Religious and political forms of tyranny will not simply disappear by educating people to be more and more knowledgeable about the relativity and partiality of all religious and political systems. The relativizing effect of historical consciousness may unmask the pretensions of church and state, but it is powerless to stop a religious fanatic like Khoumeni or a racist and nationalistic policy like apartheid. Historicism is not sufficient to save humanity, because it is in fact part of the problem; it participates in the lostness of humanity.

There is no simple way to save humanity by teaching more history to more people. In fact, historical knowledge will always undercut the believability of traditional assurances of the place, value, and significance of the individual, or of the self. The more the individual knows of history, including evolution, cosmology, psychology, sociology (especially the sociology of knowledge), the more difficult to believe that one is "a true individual." The irony here is manifest. We live in a time of heightened, some would say exaggerated, individualism;[10] people today as perhaps never before are extremely *conscious* of themselves as *individuals*, as subjects, as discrete selves centered in self-awareness, while at the same time their own historical knowledge cuts the other way and pictures them as objects, as having no identity except as products of a web of causal connections. *Individual consciousness* (the self aware of the self) is the intuition of personal uniqueness, of intrinsic value of the self: "I, a subject, matter." But the self has only the self to rely on for that confidence in the self, because at the same time *historical knowledge* catches all individuals up into a universal and objective causal system. Subjectivity disappears into objectivity. In light of what people can know about the social, cultural, biological, and historical influences which shape them, they would be hard pressed, as individuals, to sustain the belief that their own consciousness is genuinely their own, that their subjective individuality is authentic. Because it seems primarily to relativize and erode identity and to undercut the place and significance of the individual and to make persons more rather than less vulnerable to absolutistic forms of authority, historical knowledge in and of itself can scarcely be regarded as salvific.

But historical knowledge can, paradoxically, point the way to salvation. The rise of historical consciousness which has relativized everything, and particularly the place and significance of the individual or the self, nevertheless has its own history which can be traced. That is to say, in the whole history of humanity, historical consciousness is itself a *relative* phenomenon. It too, after all, has a beginning in history, and everything in history that has a beginning also has an ending. Historical consciousness which relativizes—and thus indirectly threatens—humanity is itself relative; it will end.

Historical knowledge, ironically, points to its own relativity and thus points to the hope for salvation from the destructive threat stemming from relativity. There is hope, because even historical consciousness is doomed. Indeed, the only thing that can *save humanity* is the *destruction of history* as humanity has lately come to know it.

Jesus as Total Presence

Human beings obviously were not always blessed/cursed with consciousness of historical relativity. Altizer cites a common opinion among historians of consciousness that roughly in the eighth century before Christ there was a significant break from earlier modes of awareness. This break occurred almost simultaneously in Greece in the time of Homer, and in Israel in the time of the great prophets, as well as on the subcontinent of India.[11] Until that shift in awareness occurred, human consciousness was nonindividualistic, corporate, and societal. Its mythical world—the realm of the transcendent— was not sharply distinguished from the actual world of social existence. Any vague sense of a gap between them would disappear in communal ritual. The security of the mythical world broke apart when historical awareness emerged and the heightened sense of the radically Transcendent was accompanied by the tragic sense that the gap between the actual world and the Holy can no longer be automatically overcome by ritual, that indeed the individual now stands out from the corporate as a responsible self, as a core self with greater freedom and greater risk. Ritual no longer was an assured way of salvation for the individual. Now the commitment of free and responsible selves was required. Salvation—too—was drawn into the flux and contingencies of history comprised of responsible, yet unpredictable selves. "History" began in this axial period.

Thus Altizer, instead of embracing historical relativity joyfully, analyzes the profound contradictions implied in our very consciousness of relativity. The influence of Hegel, who "created the philosophy of history," is apparent.[12] Contradictions always relativize what seems absolute. The corrosive power of historical consciousness eats away at all assurances, including the self's own individual

consciousness which was born simultaneously with historical awareness in the first place. But this, too, is passing away because historical consciousness, paradoxically, has led to the historical discovery of its own beginning in the eighth century B.C.E. It also has
led biblical scholars to identify the uniqueness of apocalyptic as the
historical *beginning of the end* of the historical era. What began
with the prophets *began to end with Jesus*. Furthermore, that beginning of the end of history is even now coming to its *fulfillment*
in our own time. Altizer writes that the so-called axial period

> was a unique historical moment when an individual form of con-
> sciousness broke through the previous collective or corporate identity
> of consciousness, and did so in such a way as to make possible a
> truly individual act and enactment of consciousness. But ours is the
> time of the end of a unique and individual consciousness, and the end
> of that consciousness is the end of history as well, and the beginning
> of a posthistorical time when an integral and interior individuality
> will have disappeared.[13]

Three questions regarding Altizer's proposal remain. First, in what
sense does the *end* of history (as relativity, individual consciousness,
threat of totalitarianism, etc.) *begin* in Jesus? Second, what evidence
is there that the end which began in Jesus is *now* being *fulfilled?*
Finally, what *new* consciousness is emerging as the *salvation* of
humanity in Jesus?

In answering the first question it becomes clear that Altizer has
a very high doctrine of the historical *finality* of Jesus, which places
the significance of Jesus beyond all historical relativity. Finality in
what sense? In the sense that in Jesus one confronts the total negation
of relativity, that Jesus is the beginning of the end of history understood in terms of individual consciousness. Recall that awareness
of relativity emerged when the realm of the transcendent was split
off from historical actuality. When the ultimate was split off from
the actual into a separation or *dualism*, the relativity of everything
actual became very manifest to consciousness. The prophetic ''Thus
says the Lord'' could then render historical events and individuals
all the more relative, problematic, and ambiguous. The end *of* history
as salvation *from* historical relativity can happen only when that
dualism (which assumes that the ultimate must be absolutely *other*

than cosmos or world) is itself destroyed. In Jesus the very dualism which goes hand in hand with all historical consciousness begins to end, and the fundamental clue for that end is the *language of Jesus,* primarily the parabolic speech of Jesus. The parables of Jesus, which are in no sense dualistic, are the verbal clue par excellence of what Altizer means by total presence as the destruction of dualism.

Parabolic speech, says Altizer, is distorted as soon as it is written down. "In this sense . . . pure parable . . . is present only in its enactment, only in its telling or saying."[14] Altizer insists that parable is unique and must not be confused with allegory, metaphor, simile, or symbol. It does not point to something else, something that is elsewhere and must somehow be represented. Parable is not a substitute or a stand-in for the real thing. Parable does not give the hearer some distance from its reality as though pointing somewhere else. Parables enact and make present; they do not act as stand-ins. When Jesus spoke the parables of the kingdom of God, the kingdom was by his parabolic speaking made present as a total presence and not as a literary picture of a dualistic Other whose reality can only be pointed to. The parables of the kingdom of God use the language of everydayness because the kingdom as "parabolic enactment occurs on earth and not in heaven. . . . Now is the time of decision, and this nowness reverses every trace of a beyond which is only beyond . . . [and] of a world which is merely and only world."[15]

Whereas other forms of speech put distance between language or voice and what is referred to—that is, they are always "about" something *else*—that distance is absent in parabolic speech. Thus the kingdom of God is *not* the subject about which the parables speak, because the kingdom is not distant from the parables. Rather, in the everydayness of parabolic speech the dualistic distance between "world" and "kingdom of God" is shattered by the immediacy of total presence, and that shattering is the beginning of the end of history.

The apocalyptic shattering of dualism, let it be noted, means the shattering of conventional ideas about God and the world as well. Most people still cling to dualistic notions: God for them is totally Other than the world and the self, even though that very dualism is the basis of historical consciousness. To be saved from historical consciousness is also to surrender the absolute otherness of God.

The total presence of God in Jesus means the end of God as totally other. Altizer comments on the difficulty of apprehending "simultaneous affirmation and negation of the world."

> The presence of the Kingdom of God is simultaneously salvation and judgement, and its fullness as salvation is inseparable from its fullness as judgement, so that the redemption of the world is simultaneously the end of the world.[16]

In other words, if God is in Jesus then "history" as understood by historical consciousness has already lost its footing and has started its plunge downward to destruction. The total presence of the kingdom of God, on the one hand, is total affirmation of the world and, on the other hand, is total judgment of the dualistic consciousness and its notions of a relativistic world under a purely transcendent God. "No such God is present in Jesus" and cannot be, because the language of Jesus "celebrates and embodies a total presence of God." Total presence, implied by the language of Jesus, is not the equivalent of pantheism. "Only a dualistic consciousness would necessarily be impelled to understand a total presence of God as a pantheistic deification of the world."[17]

In answer to our second question, Altizer finds considerable evidence that we are being hurled toward the End begun in Jesus. What guides his selection of evidence is the notion of total presence. There can be "no real final and total presence of God, apart from a negation of every other presence and identity of God." This is the offense of the eschatological Word. It means "a negation of every identity of God which is present to consciousness as God, or which stands out or apart from consciousness, or which is manifest as God and God alone."[18] Thus Altizer can say that the kingdom of God is approaching whenever and wherever the dualistic consciousness is transformed. His catalog of evidence is a roll call of philosophers, scientists, artists, poets, and musicians. Sometimes this negation and transformation of consciousness happens when apocalyptic movements break out. It happened when modern science dawned and demolished the world conceived as a hierarchically ordered whole. It can be seen in those developments in art and literature, whether of Rembrandt and Shakespeare or of Joyce and Picasso, in which apocalyptic energy embodying total presence shatters all limits of consciousness. It can be noted in the conceptual work of Hegel, Marx, and Nietzsche. Everywhere Altizer looks he sees evidence of the disintegration and negation of the bad (that is, dualistic) consciousness or personal identity. This negation is the consummation of what Jesus had set in motion.

> Already in the proclamation of Jesus, a total presence realizes and presents itself only by way of its negative assault upon all given or established identity, and it is the reversal of the center or ground of established identity which actualizes a total and final presence.[19]

Salvation as Universal Consciousness

Finally, we ask what new consciousness is being brought forth by way of radical negation. What is the nature of salvation if lostness is understood in terms of all the threats of historical relativity? If Jesus—as total presence—is the beginning of the end of history, and if "the end of history is the end of a unique and individual consciousness . . . ,"[20] what new consciousness will rise out of the ruin of history? What comes *after* history and after the triumph of Jesus over unique and individual consciousness?

Stated simply, the answer is universal consciousness. It is the new and authentic consciousness, replacing the disintegrating false individualism of modernity. The apocalyptic and total presence of Jesus hurled itself against both religion and the empire and thus initiated the end of that false consciousness which always shores itself up by, and in turn perpetuates, the false dualism of sacred and profane realms. The violent disintegration of the individual consciousness must happen if true consciousness is to supersede false consciousness. Total presence is simultaneously total judgment and total grace. This judgment—this violent dissolution of false consciousness—is also salvation in Jesus who is the pioneer of genuine, concrete universal humanity. In other words, universal consciousness emerges even as individual consciousness—which must be destroyed if humanity is to be saved—loses all definiteness and dissolves into universal consciousness.

Even now, as Western, "civilized" Christendom declines, the original proclamation of Jesus is being reborn. The death of dualistic

notions of absolute transcendence means the birth of the new consciousness which "initially realized itself by discovering the ancient
world or worlds, thereby discovering a new world of the Bible."[21]
As the new world of the Bible has been rediscovered, false consciousness rushes toward its end.

That end has already dawned in the disintegration of a pure interiority,
and as that disintegration is enacted again and again throughout the
fullest moments of our lives, a concrete universality is actually embodied among us, and even if it is impossible for an individual voice
or consciousness to name or envision that universality, it nevertheless
is true that we know that universality to be real, and know it to be
real because it is realized among us, and realized among us in the
deepest and most actual moments of our own interior disintegration.
For those are the moments when we are given another . . . who is
most distant from ourselves and above all most distant from a unique
and individual "I." . . . Only a reversal of that "I" can truly embody
presence . . . [and] that presence makes possible the embodiment of
a universal presence, and therefore the actual historical realization of
universal consciousness.[22]

Thus, universal consciousness is the salvation which was begun
in Jesus and which alone can rescue humanity from all the destructiveness heaped upon humanity by self-centered and false consciousness. Its presence cannot be named, but it can nonetheless be
known and realized.

Altizer does offer a few specific clues to what "concrete universality" might be. Surely the negation of false consciousness is the
first and major sign that universal consciousness is being realized.
And, as we have seen, it is hinted at in modern artistic expressions
which shatter individual centers of identity. It can also happen when
we lose self-consciousness in one of those rare moments when we
encounter another who is present to us as a "truly human presence"
and we lose consciousness of them as merely male or female, old
or young, black or white. "Self-consciousness is just what is missing
from all which we can know as a truly human presence." Self-
consciousness simply recedes and is not dominant in such moments.
Universal consciousness is present likewise in a moment of true and
absolute solitude, a moment no one can merely choose but which

comes upon us when we least expect it and "delivers us from everything that is only our own." Furthermore, music or meditation may be the occasion of absolute solitude and thus of total presence.

> Genuine solitude is a voyage into the interior, but it is a voyage which culminates in a loss of our interior, a loss reversing every manifest or established center of our interior so as to make possible the advent of a wholly new but totally immediate world.

American jazz is Altizer's concluding instance of the reality of universal presence. Jazz is

> the only art which is . . . fusion between an archaic spirit and modern art . . . [and] the coincidence of two racial worlds. The power embodied in jazz violently shatters our interior, as its pure rhythm both returns us to an archaic identity and hurls us into a new and posthistoric universality. Most startling of all, the "noise" of jazz releases a new silence, a silence marked by the absence of every center of selfhood, the silence of a new . . . absolute solitude which has finally negated and reversed every unique and interior ground of consciousness, thereby releasing the totality of consciousness in a total and immediate presence.[23]

Jesus as Savior, in Altizer's view, is Jesus as the pioneer of universal humanity. His Christology is similar to others examined in these chapters: it is clearly shaped by his perception of lostness. Lostness is that false consciousness which takes for granted the reality of the core self or of interiority, which in turn grasps after its own salvation but without any loss of the self. False consciousness clings ever so desperately to the illusion of the distinct self, of oneself as absolutely unique and individual. Even though the self knows that each self is limited and partial and therefore, relativistically speaking, a mere momentary pulse of activity in the totality of things, the self nevertheless grasps at the illusion of being a true individual and then needs to believe in a Christendom which reinforces that illusion. As was noted, only as this illusion, the offspring of historical-dualistic consciousness, is itself destroyed by the reality of total presence found supremely in the language/reality of Jesus, can universal consciousness be born and humanity saved.

Drawing on an apocalyptic reading of the New Testament and on Hegel, Nietzsche, and a host of poets and artists, Altizer thus affirms both the universality *and* the *exclusive finality* of Jesus, the Christ of total presence.

From Christocentrism to Theocentricism

We have been considering Altizer's provocative proposal that humanity can be saved only by crushing false individual consciousness and along with it "history" as it has been conceived, and that it was precisely that destruction/salvation which was begun in Jesus as the total presence of God. A new universal consciousness is emerging as even now the old particularistic consciousness is being demolished by the total presence. Christianity alone knows this Word, namely, that that which first happened in Jesus—and in no other—is now being fulfilled.

Some Catholic and Protestant thinkers are also calling for a more universal theological outlook, but they would be offended by the exclusivistic term "Christianity alone" (even apart from the radical implications of Altizer's rejection of the absolute transcendence of God). They wish to reject or at least to modify phrases such as "Christ alone" or "Christianity alone" or "outside the church there is no salvation" (*extra ecclesiam nulla salus*). They bolster their challenges to exclusivism with biblical, theological, and historical arguments, but the urgency with which they press their cause—in short, their motive—in most instances comes from the fact that more than ever before Christians are confronted by other great world religions.

One prominent figure challenging Christocentrism is John Hick. He, too, refers back to the eighth century B.C.E. as the turning point in human awareness. "The golden age of religious creativity" was not only the time in Palestine of the early Jewish prophets, but also in Persia of Zoroaster, in China of Lao-tzu and then Confucius, in India of the Upanishads and the Buddha and, toward the end of the period, the writing of the Bhagavad Gita; furthermore, at this time Greece produced Pythagoras and, later, Socrates and Plato. Hick's bold suggestion is that *all* of these were "moments of divine revelation." The instant communication of the modern era was not available, and so none of these local revelations became known on a worldwide basis. For the most part, the several cultures in which, almost simultaneously, revelation had occurred, were ignorant of one another. By the time the several religious movements had expanded to the extent that their boundaries touched each other, they were already consolidated as world faiths which have never been able to penetrate one another to any important degree. None of them, however, had a simple, uncontested history, and some have declined. They have all undergone transformations as they have encountered other traditions.

This historical context, Hick insists, should make it clear that the differing religious traditions are not mutually exclusive and that it is then "intelligible historically why the revelation of the divine reality to man . . . had to occur separately within the several streams of human life."[24] In other words, it is perfectly clear *that* the many world religions erupted at roughly the same time (assuming, of course, that both Christianity and Islam are later, albeit distinctive offshoots, of Old Testament religion). But *why* they are different and why they make conflicting truth claims when all are moments of divine revelation is simply answered: "the ultimate divine reality" cannot be perfectly grasped by limited human minds or "encompassed by human thought," a point made in all the major religious traditions. This should not be taken to mean that any and all conceptions of the divine are valid. Each tradition has its own tests or requirements for how the divine reality can be legitimately and properly spoken of or addressed. For instance, the long history of prayer and worship in any tradition will itself test whether this or that conception of the divine can truly sustain the faith of that tradition. No doctrine would have endured if it had not the power to sustain the faith of that tradition.

The *differences* in doctrine are historically explainable, in part, by the cultural circumstances. For instance, if Christianity had expanded eastward into India and not primarily westward into the Graeco-Roman culture, its doctrines or intellectual interpretations of Jesus as the way to salvation would have been different. Faith in Jesus as Savior can be sustained in a given culture only if Christian doctrines about Christ reflect the dominant ways of thinking. In India Christianity would have encountered a culture in which

Buddhism was then becoming a powerful influence and the Mahayana doctrines were being developed, [and] it is likely that instead of Jesus being identified as the divine logos or the divine Son he would have been identified as a Bodhisattva who, like Gotama some four centuries earlier, had attained to Buddhahood or perfect relationship to reality, but had in compassion for suffering mankind voluntarily lived out his human life in order to show others the way to salvation.[25]

Doubtless, many Christians would view such a Buddhistic interpretation of Jesus as not merely different but absolutely wrong, even heretical. But Hick's point is that doctrine does develop in a cultural context; it could have developed differently but for the historical accident that Christianity expanded first into the Graeco-Roman culture. To regard the Western interpretation of Jesus as the one and only correct interpretation, and not merely as a different interpretation, is to elevate what is accidental and nonessential to the status of what is absolute and essential.

Hick contends that the exclusivistic claim is not really essential to Christianity, but is itself a historical development of Western imperialistic Christianity and not of the essence of Christianity. He likens it to the claim that the earth is the center of the universe itself, the Ptolemaic concept which had to be abandoned for the Copernican concept in order better to accommodate what was being observed in the universe. So Hick supports what he calls "the Copernican Revolution in theology," an equally radical transformation in one's conception of the universe of world faiths and of the relative position of one's own religious tradition in that universe. This revolution

> involves a shift from the dogma that Christianity is at the centre to the realization that it is *God* who is at the center, and that all the religions of mankind, including our own, serve and revolve around him.[26]

From Particularism to Universality

Theology has been moving away from extreme Christocentrism. Thus, Paul Tillich, in his own reflections on Christianity's encounter with the world religions, observed that throughout its history the rhythm of criticism, countercriticism, and self-criticism has marked

Christianity's encounter with not only polytheism, but also Greek religion, mysticism, and other faiths. Christianity has demonstrated a capacity to receive external criticism from other traditions, to counter it, and then to transform that criticism into self-criticism. As a result of its modern encounter with world religions—another instance of that rhythm—contemporary Christianity is moving away from attempts at "conversion" toward a "community of conversation" among the religious traditions. Christianity itself is being transformed as it breaks through its own particularism to universality, which is that "point at which religion itself loses its importance."[27]

John Hick represents the extreme move away from particularistic Christocentrism. For him the claim that Jesus is the *only* Savior is not essential to Christianity. Biblical scholarship does not support the idea that Jesus made such claims for himself. That doctrine was developed by the church and was already insinuated into the New Testament as the theological interpretation of the writers. The nub of Hick's position is that exclusivistic and Christocentric claims should be given up—because they are nonessential—in favor of that which *is* essential. At its core Christianity is a way of salvation originating in Jesus Christ, but its future as *a* way of salvation is dependent on whether people find salvation in it. The test is soteriological. Simply put, Christianity "will continue as a way of salvation so long as men and women continue to find salvation—that is spiritual life and health—through it."[28] The viability of Christianity as a way of salvation is not guaranteed. As a historical religion it, too, has failed and—if it does not complete the Copernican revolution in its own theology—will fail again. A Christianity that is centered on itself and on an exclusivistic understanding of salvation in Christ alone will simply fail to be a way of salvation. Exclusivistic claims do not uphold or defend the saving work of Christ, but in practice frustrate, contradict, and deny it.

It is primarily as a philosopher of religion that Hick raises his objections to Christian exclusivism. We will also indicate briefly the objections of two theologians, Karl Rahner and Paul Knitter, as well as the critical view of a scholar of world religions, Wilfred Cantwell Smith.

John Hick, the philosopher, looks upon Christian claims from a somewhat detached perspective. As noted, he thinks that Christianity can still be effective as one of the great religions of the world if it gives up its exclusivistic claims to be the *only* way of salvation. For Hick, then, the central fact of Christianity, indeed the essence of Christianity, is that Jesus of Nazareth was and is experienced as Savior and can still be so experienced, but Hick's caution is that we "should therefore not infer, from the Christian experience of redemption through Christ, that salvation cannot be experienced in any other way." He put the same point in another context:

> We have in the end to say something like this: All salvation—that is, all creating of human animals into children of God—is the work of God. The different religions have their different name for God acting savingly towards mankind. . . . But what we cannot say is that all who are saved are saved by Jesus of Nazareth.

When Christianity tries to exclude *other* ways in the name of bolstering the Christian way the effect is to undercut the very essence of Christianity. It is of the essence of Christianity that *for Christians* Jesus is *the* revelation of God's will for the world. In Jesus Christians find *all* the evidence that is essential for *them* to believe that God acts savingly toward humanity, but when they deny that God is acting savingly in other religions they effectively blunt the essential point of Christianity.[29]

Theologians, too, have tried to find a position that will affirm the distinctiveness and uniqueness of the saving work of Jesus Christ but without rejecting the genuinely salvific value of other great religions. In addition to Rahner and Knitter, Hans Küng and Raimundo Panikkar of the Catholic community, and Don Cupitt, John Macquarrie, John B. Cobb Jr., Tom Driver, and J. A. T. Robinson in the Protestant community, are among the best known.[30] The "Declaration on the Relation of the Church to Non-Christian Religions" of Vatican II exhibits this same spirit. The declaration recognizes that Hindus "seek liberation from the constrictions of this world by various forms of asceticism, deep meditation or loving and trustful recourse to God" and that Buddhists "are taught how with confident application they can achieve a state of complete liberation, or reach the highest level of illumination, either through their own efforts or with help from above." Rejecting nothing that is true in any of these other ways, the Catholic church respects them and, even though

these other ways may differ from the teachings of the Catholic tradition, they "often reflect the brightness of that Truth which is the
light of all men."[31]

A significant point of consensus here is that the Christian confession of Jesus as *the* one in whom *Christians* find wholeness,
health, salvation, and unity with God is no warrant for supposing
that there is no salvific worth in *other* religions. Indeed, writes Karl
Rahner in his famous essay, "Christianity and Other Religions,"
because of the gospel and

> contrary to every merely human experience, we do have every reason
> for thinking optimistically of God and his salvific will . . . [and] we
> have every right to suppose that grace has not only been offered even
> outside the Christian Church . . . but also that, in a great many cases
> at least, grace gains the victory . . . .[32]

The possibility that the saving grace of God, which Christians
know and trust because of Jesus, can actually win the heart of a
non-Christian *apart* from explicit knowledge of Jesus of Nazareth
led Rahner in the same essay to espouse his now-famous doctrine
of the "anonymous Christian." He did not mean to affirm that a
person is in actuality a confessing Christian even though he or she
has never heard the gospel, but he intended by the use of the term
to affirm and emphasize the universality of grace which is operative
in the lives of all people apart from explicit knowledge of the historical Jesus of Nazareth. It is a presumption of Christian faith, says
Rahner, that while there is no other salvation than Christ's salvation,
that salvation is effective even before a person makes an explicitly
Christian confession of faith in Jesus as Savior. The Christian simply
cannot renounce that presumption because "it is a profound admis-
sion of the fact that God is greater than man and the Church."[33]

Rahner's doctrine of the anonymous Christian, while it moves
away from exclusivity, nevertheless does imply Christian superiority. It means that, although other ways of salvation than Christian
ones are genuine and come as gifts from the God of grace whom
Christians know in Christ, they are nonetheless incomplete, and that
the Christian way, while not the only way, is the ultimate way and
thus superior to other ways.

The implied claim for the superiority of the Christian way is troublesome to theologians like Paul Knitter, also a Roman Catholic, who thinks that Rahner's proposal does not go far enough toward a genuinely theocentric Christology. Knitter insists that although Rahner and others, like the process theologian John Cobb,[34] have gone beyond a church-centered approach to salvation, theirs is still a Christocentric and not a theocentric Christology. Knitter's own proposal hinges principally on a linguistic strategy, namely, to make a distinction between confessional language and the language of philosophy, logic, and especially of theology. Taking his clue from Krister Stendahl and Frances Young, Knitter thinks that when the scripture writers expressed themselves in terms of "Jesus only" they were writing more as committed lovers who exaggerate in order to protest their undying devotion to the one and only beloved than as philosophers reflecting abstractly on the meaning of being in love with only one among several possible lovers. Phrases like "no other name" and "Jesus only" are the language of the heart and not of the head, and one should not confuse the two. With this distinction Knitter hopes to show the continuing value—as "heart" language—of exclusive terms, but then to resist pressing this kind of confessional language to the limits of "head" language, that is, to the point of theologically and theoretically excluding other ways in which God, the great Lover, may have acted to save humanity.[35] Thus, when one speaks confessionally, one is justified in retaining the appropriate language of exclusivity as the mark of true devotion to the Christian way, but one cannot legitimately go further and imply theologically that the Christian way is superior to, or exclusive of, other ways.

Knitter offers an explanation for the persistent habit of Christian thinkers in pressing the exclusiveness of commitment language (the first order speech of faith) to its illogical and even contradictory consequences in theological language (the second order speech of reflection and thought). He offers three explanatory observations. First, Christian theology developed its exclusivistic Christology in the "classicist culture" of the Graeco-Roman world in which it was trying to defend the *truth* of the Christian way. Unlike the relativist views of our own "historical culture," the formative classicist culture, Knitter declares, assumed that truth was one, certain, fixed, and normative. Theologians in the classicist culture had no choice: to claim the truth of the Christian way meant that one was obliged to argue that it was the one and only, the final and exclusive way. Second, first generation Christians were infected by the Jewish eschatological mentality of the time. To have experienced as they did that in Jesus the kingdom of God had come upon them could *only* mean that the End of history was imminent; there simply was no time for any other revelation. Even if such had been conceivable, it was clear to the Christian community that now, in light of the End, other manifestations of God's grace were simply impossible. Finally, the early Christian community was an embattled, often persecuted, frequently misunderstood, and, in many places, outlawed religion; therefore, for sheer survival the church had to be absolutely clear, certain, unwavering, and uncompromising in its identity. Its Christological beliefs had to be stated in absolute terms and without equivocation in order to steel the community against the ridicule and persecution of the culture.[36] Absolutist theology has always seemed more helpful to Christians in times of threat. In ancient church history its survival value is obvious.

None of these three conditions seems uniformly applicable to the church in the last decades of the 20th century. Most educated Christians recognize that the "classicist culture" no longer prevails, and therefore should realize that a defense of the truth of Christian faith must be carried on in terms of an open, evolutionary, historical, and pluralist theory of truth. Nor do they have a naive first-century apocalyptic view of history; many, if not most, Christians think that even if it seemed certain that the Bomb would destroy civilization tomorrow, they would still be responsible for the care of children and of the vulnerable and for the planting of trees and crops. Finally, even though persecution can always erupt against courageous believers who stand for justice in totalitarian regimes or who work for equality in racist societies, Christians today can also point to impressive gains in religious freedom in large parts of the world and to free societies where the church's ministry is a welcome contribution to the commonwealth and is not perceived as a threat to the civil order. In short, the historical reasons which compelled earlier Christians to bolster faith in Jesus as Savior with an absolutist and exclusivist Christology no longer dominate present-day Christianity.

Jesus as Mediator of Religious Conflict

Christian thinkers who call for a more God-centered Christology do not intend to demote the person and work of Christ to a lower rank. A Christology centered in God does not necessarily make less of *Christ's* relationship to the *divine* reality at all, but it does alter how Christ is understood to relate to other religious *expressions* of the divine. These theologians think that nothing other than Jesus' ministry, death, and resurrection (which cannot be separated from their effect on believers) should determine how Christians understand God, because for *Christians* Jesus was and is *the* instance of a human life centered on and determined by God. *Theocentric Christology is derived from the theocentric Jesus.* Incarnation should mean at least that much. A theocentric Christology, these theologians would argue, is authorized by the God-centered Jesus and completely reverses the understandable but unfortunate and dangerous Christology which implies that God is so exclusively centered on Jesus that the saving grace of God operates only where the name of Jesus is proclaimed or the church ministers in that name.

A practical result of this position is this: if in the day-by-day theology of Christians it were really Jesus, the God-centered one, who determines how they conceive of God's relation to all humankind, then Christians could let go of, and indeed reverse, any lingering imperialistic attitude which assumes that God is centered only in Jesus and cannot be savingly present in other religions. Christian arrogance would probably be less prevalent. Wilfred Cantwell Smith, Harvard Professor of Comparative Religion, doubtless has empirical grounds for the following statement:

> It is my observation over more than twenty years of study of the Orient, and a little now of Africa, that the fundamental flaw of Western civilization in its role in world history is arrogance, and that this has infected also the Christian Church. If you think that I am being reckless and unwarranted here, ask any Jew, or read between the lines of the works of modern African or Asian thinkers.[37]

Obviously, Smith believes that arrogance is an infection which the church has picked up through its close association with Western cultures, but also, as a scholar of religions, he knows that doctrine can intensify such infections in a religious tradition. He is shocked by what he calls the "morally un-Christian" reaction of some people who cannot rejoice in the pious and moral life of Muslims or Buddhists, Jews or Hindus. Exclusivistic views of salvation always lead Christians to the anxiety-inducing conclusion that if a neighbor were to know unity or closeness with God through a non-Christian faith, then Christianity must be fallacious. The alternative which Professor Smith and others propose is to challenge that exclusivistic premise. Smith himself is not a theologian, at least in the usual sense of the term, but he does offer an alternative proposal which places him very close to others considered in this chapter. His own prescription is that the infection of arrogance can be cured with a different, nonexclusivist Christology. He opines

> that the final doctrine on this matter may perhaps run along the lines of affirming that a Buddhist who is saved, or a Hindu or a Muslim or whoever, is saved and is saved only [sic], because God is the kind of God whom Jesus Christ has revealed him to be. . . . We are not saved by our knowledge; we are not saved by our membership in the Church; we are not saved by anything of *our* doing. We are saved, rather, by the only thing that could possibly save us, the anguish and the love of God.[38]

These authors—Hick, Rahner, Knitter, Smith, along with a growing number of others—have issued a summons to Christians to rethink Jesus as Savior in light of world religions. Some who share their concern believe that the widespread awareness of religious pluralism is as great a challenge to Christian theology as the rise of science, "that the impact of agnostic science will turn out to be as child's play to the challenge to Christian theology of the faith of other men."[39] Just as scientific discoveries about the origin of the universe required reformulations of the doctrine of creation lest the fallacy of a six-day creation render the Christian faith unbelievable, so also the discovery that people of other faiths know something of salvation will require a reformulation of Christology—indeed a universal Christ—lest "the fallacy of relentless exclusivism" lead to the conclusion that God who acts graciously and savingly in Jesus Christ is truly gracious only in a sense so limited and constricted as to undercut what Christians, because of Jesus, believe about God.

An adequate theology of the God-centered, universal Christ has yet to be written. Much of the work in this area is restricted to the preliminary task of establishing appropriate rules for interreligious conversation and cooperation. There does seem to be agreement, however, on a tenet similar to that which we found among liberation theologians, that theology is the second step.

In the case of thinkers being considered in this chapter, the first step is that Christian theologians gain knowledge of other religions. Theologians who are ignorant of other religions are as obsolete and as damaging to the cause of theology as those who in the past rejected Galileo, Newton, Darwin, or Einstein, or who today are unaware of the impact of existentialism or of Marxism on the minds and sensibilities of people. The first step, for the sake of an adequate Christology for this religiously pluralistic age, entails putting aside anything in traditional Christology which hinders or discourages genuine and appreciative knowledge of the salvific ways of other religions, just as the first step in liberation theology entails putting aside anything in traditional Christology which hinders Christians from associating with sinners, outcasts, the poor, and the oppressed.

The first step, in other words, is to come as close as possible to believing in other religions, at least as close as possible both to knowing and to understanding *from within* what it is to be a Buddhist, or a Muslim, or a Jew, or a Hindu. This would involve "passing over" into the faith-world of the other, using whatever imaginative clues are available to know and to understand that faith-world from its center, and then to "come back."[40] Of course, such an exercise in learning by immersion will not leave a Christian unchanged. The point is that one "passes over" as a Christian and comes back still a Christian, but now transformed; that it is only *after* that transformation takes place that an appropriate Christology can be written as the second step. Just as liberation theologians do advocate immersion in social action as an act of faith in Christ who liberates from social injustice, the implication here too is that committing oneself to immersion in another religion is an act of faith in Christ as the one who mediates religious conflict.

Those who are committed to Christ as the one who meets them in other religions as mediator of religious conflict are similar to those who are committed to Christ as the one who meets them among the poor and despised as the liberator from oppression. The second step, theological reflection on religious or political immersions, will inevitably produce a Christology quite different from any that would have been constructed without the first step.

According to theocentric proposals, Christ, the God-centered Jesus, calls all people to follow him not only into the struggle for justice but also into the interreligious quest for a universal humanity. *That* Christology, developed in conversation with other faiths, has yet to be constructed. It would be demeaning to predict that it will be necessary to diminish faith in Christ, to water down Christianity, to make it compatible with any and all religions. Interreligious conversation requires greater, not less, trust in Christ, because Christ calls believers to forsake the secure ghetto of Christian particularism and to join the interreligious quest for the unity which goes beyond the grasp of local Christianity and beyond even its finest Christologies. As Panikkar has put it, "It is precisely because I take seriously Christ's affirmation that he is the way, the truth, and the life, that I cannot reduce his significance only to historical Christianity."[41]

As one religion among many, the church's charter on salvation is a limited franchise, not a monopoly.

Chapter Six

THE ANONYMOUS CHRIST: A CONSTRUCTIVE CHRISTOLOGY FOR POSTMODERN CHRISTIANS

The Ambiguity of Belief and Betrayal

Faith in Jesus has driven Christians deeply into every culture and nation in the world. Faith has compelled them to learn the languages, philosophies, folkways, and the religious beliefs of others in order to communicate the good news that Jesus is God's way of redeeming the world. The apostolic imperative to preach to all nations meant that Christians have had to learn to think, speak, and act as others think, speak, and act, so that as Christians their thoughts, speech, and actions—informed by, but not conformed to, the ways of the world—might communicate what it means to be redemptively transformed by new life in Christ. Faith opened early Christians to the necessity and the possibility of rendering the gospel's truth in the categories of Greek philosophy. The great achievement of classical Christianity was its accommodation to and creative use of Graeco-Roman culture. Its classic formulations not only commended the faith to the culture but also preserved the faith against heresy. In the modern period, however, the urgent question has been how to liberate the gospel from old patterns of thought without losing the truth which those old patterns were able to communicate and conserve for many centuries.[1]

Faith still drives believers deeply into Latin American cultures, into the pluralism of North America, into the ancient ways of the Orient, into African struggles for independence, and into conversation with other religions. The immersion of believers in the diversity of environments is full of risks. Believers can unwittingly betray the One whose truth they want to bring to others. Sometimes betrayal takes the form of totally adapting to their environment. In learning to speak, think, and act as Americans, Christians have sometimes confused piety with uncritical patriotism. Betrayal can also take the form of living within the walls of a "Christian" compound in deep suspicion of the philosophy or religion of the surrounding culture. Christians have sometimes confused evangelism with isolation from the world, taking the natives out of their culture and into a spiritualized zone separate from the world of their birth. Both strategies are now recognized as betrayals of belief. The irony lies in the fact that belief and betrayal are closely related; hence ambiguity abounds.

The ambiguity is not a modern discovery. The New Testament drama of salvation itself warns us that the most fervent disciple can betray Jesus, and that what seems—by the standards of human wisdom—a betrayal of moral goals and expectations can be a shocking revelation of the generosity of God. The classic instance is the confrontation between Jesus and Peter at Caesarea Philippi, as told in Matthew 16 and parallels. When asked directly by Jesus, "Who do you say that I am?" Simon's response, "You are the Christ, the Son of the living God," earned him the name by which he is remembered—Peter the Rock. A few verses later Jesus rebuked the believing Peter and called him "Satan"—the supreme betrayer—for his refusal to accept what Jesus saw as the outcome of his own ministry. In Peter's view, for Jesus to predict his own death was defeatism. His death would betray all that Peter had expected when he gave up his fishing business and signed on as a follower. It was later—after he had denied Jesus three more times and after the execution scene from which he had fled—that something entirely different became clear to him. Peter came to see that by accepting death, Jesus had not *betrayed* the kingdom; indeed, by his death Jesus *opened* the kingdom of heaven to all believers, even to the uncircumcised whom Peter had thought unworthy and unclean (Acts 10 and 11). Because he felt betrayed by Jesus, Peter was led into betrayal himself. But if the mission of salvation were to be accomplished, it was necessary for Jesus to accept death and thus to betray Peter's earlier hopes and expectations.

The apostolic witness, then, is a warning that even the belief of an apostle does not guarantee against acting as a betrayer, as a traitor who hands the truth over to the enemy of truth. The Scripture's report of Jesus saying to Peter, the chief apostle, "You are Satan," is a clear warning that belief in Jesus can take Satanic forms. Not everyone who believes, not everyone who says, "Lord, Lord," shall enter the kingdom of heaven, and some who do enter will be surprised, as the parable of the great judgment makes clear: "Then the righteous will answer him, 'Lord when did we see thee hungry . . . or thirsty . . . a stranger . . . or naked . . . sick or in prison. . . .?' And the King will answer them, 'Truly . . . as you did it to one of the least of these my brethren, you did it to me' " (Matt. 25:31ff.). There is much in Scripture to warn believers to be everlastingly alert to the ambiguity of their own belief.

The scriptural testimony to the ambiguity of belief has a counterpart that many Christians would point to as their most favored of all Bible passages: "For God so loved the world that he gave his only Son, that whoever believes in him should not perish but have eternal life" (John 3:16). In such texts there seems to be little ambiguity. Salvation is tied quite directly to belief that Jesus is the *only* (no ambiguity there) Son.

> For God sent the Son into the world, not to condemn the world, but that the world might be saved through him. Whoever believes in him is not condemned; those who do not believe are condemned already, because they have not believed in the name of the only Son of God (vv. 17-18 RSV alt.).

The dramatic warnings about belief and betrayal do not, of course, blunt the central unambiguous point of these and similar texts. The ambiguity lies not at all in those texts but in believers who repeatedly confuse their witness to the Savior with the Savior to whom they witness. That which is to be believed (that Jesus is Savior) cannot be surpassed and must never be compromised, but *how* that belief is expressed in doctrine, or communicated to others, or defended against opponents will always be an open question.[2]

The Plurality of Secondary Criteria

In previous chapters I have tried to make clear just how open is the question of theological expression of belief in Jesus as Savior among 20th-century Christian thinkers. My own presentation of the many ways of interpreting the experienced fact of Jesus as Savior has stressed what is compelling and persuasive about each one. Throughout, I have restricted critical comment about any of them to what other theologians have offered, for instance, Tillich against Barth, or John Hick against Christocentrism. All of them catch something of the truth, just as none has exhausted all the truth. Every serious theology is a witness to the truth; none is itself the truth. Therefore, a theology is a witness whose testimony is given in faith—under oath, so to say. Theologians owe to each other a respectful hearing, even if several disagree among themselves and perhaps offend some cherished notions. It is the case that all of the Christological testimonies of the 20th century have gained some prominence in certain regions of the church or in certain times of urgency, yet none of them has been exempt from fair and sound criticism. Certainly no one of them can be the norm for judging all the others. The *ultimate* judgment on every Christology cannot be made on the basis of any one of those being judged. Ultimately, the criterion for a *final* judgment on the many testimonies will be that of the parable of the last judgment: *has this or that Christology hindered or helped the saving work of Christ?*

Meanwhile, penultimate or secondary criteria are available for evaluating the various Christologies proposed in this century. These secondary criteria are like the agreed-upon rules for a colloquy. They are necessarily somewhat tentative and open to revision by mutual consent and are akin to what more and more theologians take for granted, namely, that theology is dialogical or conversational. Any theological witness is relative to the context in which it occurs. As Scripture itself is best understood in light of the social context in which certain issues arose and which shaped the imagery and influenced the thought forms used to communicate the apostolic witness,[3] theological reflection similarly calls for a range of rules or criteria depending on the nature of the context in which it occurs.

David Tracy has distinguished the several rules best suited to theological conversations in various settings. For example, because the principal audience for *systematic theology* is the church or the community of believers, the criteria which are suited to that audience stress continuity with tradition and fidelity to its Scripture and creeds. The chief consideration is whether the interpretation offered by a systematic theology serves the proclamation of the church. Faithfulness to the tradition guides systematic theology. Barth's *Church Dogmatics* is an unparalleled instance of work which meets the criteria of systematic theology.

When the primary audience shifts away from the believing community, the church, to the academic community, the university, then the criteria are those which more properly fit the task of *fundamental theology*. In that context theology must respond to the challenges of philosophers, of scientists, historians, anthropologists, and linguists, among others. Rather than being primarily or principally occupied with the issues of continuity with the tradition, the question now is whether there is any continuity between theology, as one intellectual discipline, and other modes of human inquiry. The criteria for judging fundamental theology are the standards of coherence to the mind more than, but certainly not excluding, fidelity to the tradition. It would count against fundamental theology, and therefore against the Christian claim for the truth of Christ, if little or nothing of significance about Christian truth claims fell within the boundaries of what intelligent, educated persons—believers and nonbelievers alike—could agree upon as making rational, intelligible, and coherent sense. The Christologies of Tillich and Cobb have some obvious similarities here.

The corresponding audience for *practical theology* is primarily neither the ecclesiastical community nor the academic community but the society as a whole, and particularly those in society whose principal interest is not whether a theology is faithful to the tradition or appeals to the mind of elite intellectuals, but whether and to what extent theology can make any real difference in removing oppression of the poor, or improving the quality of life here and now, or overcoming the isolation of persons in society.[4]

It is more difficult to distinguish the criteriological emphases appropriate to the work of theologians like Altizer or Knitter. The audience whom these theologians seek to engage is not so discreetly identifiable as the other three. Indeed, the audience is global and the concern here is to hold on to the truth of Christ while avoiding any semblance of a dualistic consciousness or of the exclusivistic religious arrogance commonly found among Westerners. Certainly, the criterion of socioethical consequence is strongly represented in theologians like Ruether and Driver, while Knitter, Smith, and Hick think it no longer makes sense, in an evolutionary and pluralistic world, to use absolutistic, exclusivistic theories of truth in order to defend faith in Jesus. Rahner, Tillich, Cobb, and Panikkar pursue the more traditional concern that in some way Christ be the final *norm* for how God acts savingly in the world, lest salvation be strictly limited to those who believe in Jesus as the Christ. Of course, some who reject "theocentric" Christology are nevertheless sensitive to the charge of arrogance while still arguing that only a "proclaimed Christ" can offer a version of universality which is genuinely Christian—that is, Christocentric—and which does not compromise the integrity of Christianity.[5]

Plurality and Ultimate Salvation: An Evaluative Summary

The wide diversity of interpretations of Jesus is a fact; it is a reality with which any knowledgeable Christian must live in the 20th century. In previous chapters I have sorted out Christological variations according to the diversity of ways that the theologians in question perceive the human predicament of lostness. I have very briefly described, above, the several secondary criteria or norms by which to evaluate each for its relative adequacy: For the sake of proclamation, is any given interpretation *faithful,* as measured by the norms of the tradition? For the sake of apologetic defense, is it *intelligible,* as gauged by the norms of reason? For the sake of the neighbor's welfare, is it *effective,* as measured by the norms of social justice? For the sake of universal humanity (i.e., for the sake of understanding ultimacy as genuinely experienced to some degree in other faiths), is it *fair-minded and knowledgeable,* as measured by the standards of those traditions? Obviously, even this way of sorting out and evaluating diversity of interpretations is an interpretation too, and as such can only be judged as more or less adequate according to other criteria that one might propose. Nevertheless, whatever approach one might take in assessing the plurality of interpretations, the *plurality* itself is a present-day *fact* which another interpretation could never eliminate nor explain away, but could only confirm by adding to the plurality.

Can one hold to the view that all these Christologies are at least *partially* successful in communicating the *ultimate* meaning and reality of *Jesus as Savior?* Theologians have proposed Christologies (Who was Jesus?) which they believe are relevant to the dimensions of lostness which they think are painfully evident (What is salvation?). Thus Barth's Christology of Christ as the Word is particularly cogent for exposing those idolatrous tendencies in Western bourgeois culture which in some cases led Christians to embrace Hitler, and for proposing instead that only God is worthy of human loyalty—the God who is totally other and who calls all humanity to forsake false gods and to trust the One who absolutely transcends all mere cultural or religious beliefs. Jesus as the Word is a Christology which has clearly demonstrated its efficacy for winning people away—for saving them—from illusory, transitory, and idolatrous loyalties which subvert God's intention for the world.

In like manner one must notice that Pannenberg's Christology, for all of its emphasis on the historically verifiable resurrection of Jesus, is his proposal for answering the problem of history, and any cogency it has is derived from how well one thinks it addresses the nagging predicament of sheer historical contingency and relativity. The "salvation history" of the Bible can no longer be regarded as the only way to read the history of the world for clues that will bolster genuine hope for history's outcome. The Bible's "salvation history" has been challenged, and therefore relativized, by the Enlightenment. For many people the "prescientific" or "mythical"— and thus incredible—Bible story has been replaced by scientific knowledge, technical know-how, and advanced social ideals. In addition, the Marxist-Leninist view, as a competitive "salvation history," is critical of both the biblical view and the liberal-bourgeois version of the Enlightenment view, and has captured the imagination of millions.[6] These several ways of viewing history have made it impossible for many to view the whole of history with a naive hope inspired by the Bible's narrow strand of history. No limited strand of past history—no single "salvation history"—can overcome the relativity implied by the many strands of history. Pannenberg's ingenious resolution is to present Christ as the Absolute Future or End proleptically revealed in the resurrection of Jesus. Jesus—as the End—is the Christ who alone can save, because all histories are drawn toward their *telos* in him. Whether or not one accepts Pannenberg's rather astonishing view depends largely on whether the human predicament is perceived as hopelessness—made all the more desperate by the historical awareness that every "salvation history," including the Christian one, has been radically relativized.

Instead of emphasizing the category of history as the device for laying bare the human predicament, Tillich drew upon the idea of existence and its counterpart, Being. All beings have lost their original union with essential being; all are alienated and estranged. Tillich's impact on my own thinking and preaching occurred when it became clear that for me and many others the art and the literature of anxiety and despair expressed the experience of brokenness far better than traditional religious language, which had lost its power to communicate the message of Scripture. Tillich taught us to look to modern artists and writers, to existentialism, and to depth psychology for materials with which to build a bridge between the tradition and the modern age of anxiety. Estrangement, which in Tillich's thought is more than a subjective mood, corrupts all the objective structures of existence. All beings, all entities within the structures of time and space, of causal connectedness and bodiliness, are deeply flawed. If Jesus is to be grasped as the Christ who saves, then somehow Jesus must be presented as the New Being in whom all the flaws, all the marks of estrangement are overcome.

It should be obvious that much of the appeal of Tillich's Christology requires that we share his perception of the faults which go all the way to the depths of existence, shaking the very foundations of creation. Yet in spite of his elaborate and dynamic doctrine of the Spirit, Tillich's ontological scheme—his philosophy of being— seems to require that in order to be saved from the threats of nonbeing, all creatures must be drawn away from, even out of, existence into union with Being beyond existence. God, for Tillich, is ultimately unaffected by the world and does not interact with the creation. And the New Being, as Tillich portrays the Christ, is more a transparent window through which to espy God, the totally other, than the man in whom God is actively incarnate. In fact, all dialectical theology, from Barth's uncompromising proclamation to Tillich's more accommodating apologetic, stresses the absolute otherness of God. It has its strongest appeal for those who perceive the "world" and the "self" as utterly bereft of divinity so that, in order for God to become human and thus to save the godless world, the incarnation is necessarily an absolute exception to all other events because, after all, a godless world offers no analogies for anticipating and receiving an incarnation of the Word or of the New Being.

John Cobb and other process theologians deny that either Scripture or common experience, when adequately interpreted, require that God and the world be thought of in so dualistic a fashion. Using the categories of process philosophy, Cobb reconceives Jesus as the God-man in a way that does not require the *specific* incarnation of God in Jesus to be exceptional in every respect to God's *ordinary* way of relating to the world. In sharp contrast to dialectical theology, Cobb and others emphasize the doctrine of creation. God as creator is actively involved in every event of the universe, and as such is the *only agent* who is a *necessary cause for everything* that happens, but *not* the only causal agent involved *in anything* that happens. Creation implies that God is incarnate in the entire world and that God's saving activity in Jesus is a unique instance of God's will and action in history, but God-in-Jesus is not in every respect an exception to *how* God is actively present in the world. This shift of emphasis from the Second Article to the First, of course, does not have the proclamatory "bite" and "over-againstness" of dialectical theology, because it does not assume that the world is utterly "godless." If one did not believe in Jesus Christ one would still have the creation, which—however fallen it is—continues to testify to the glory of God.

Therefore, Christologies like Cobb's have the strongest appeal when our question is not confined exclusively to a Lutheran's agonizing plea, "How can I—so caught up as I am in my own despair and unbelief—find a gracious God?" Rather, the cogency of a process Christology has been sharpest when we have asked, "How does God, whose saving grace is unsurpassably disclosed and defined in Jesus, *also* work savingly within *nature* and *other* cultures and other religions?" When that question comes to the fore, without excluding the question of justification so central to St. Paul and to the Reformation, then the new conceptual system offered by process theology is a more persuasive and convincing way to relate Christology to the critical questions raised by ecology, economics, and world religions.

Some liberation theologians and many activist Christians would at this point express their impatience. Even if a philosophical theology like Tillich's or Cobb's solves some of the intellectual problems inherent in orthodoxy, such discussions are remote and have no immediate relevance for the majority in the world who are poor. Let us talk about these matters eventually, they might say, but not until we have been thoroughly immersed in the specific, complex, seemingly intractable problems of the poor, the disenfranchised, and the oppressed.

We can scarcely read the theologians of liberation or their North American colleagues, the feminist and black theologians, and not be drawn into their sense of moral urgency which is perhaps the key to the powerful appeal of their theology. Theology which produces nothing but more theology and whose only influence on action is to discourage action, seems to them to be positively immoral, regardless of how orthodox or existentially gripping it may otherwise be. Jesus would cast such theology in the role of the priest and the Levite who, out of anxiety for their own religious propriety, "passed by on the other side" and thus failed to help the man who had fallen among robbers (Luke 10:25ff.). His parable simply notes that a man whose religious beliefs in many circles would be scandalous (he was a Samaritan) went to extraordinary lengths to help the victim. When confronted with need, nothing is more urgent than that the needy be served; in *that* situation and for *that* purpose it is irrelevant whether the deed was performed by a despised Samaritan or a despised Marxist.

The experience of salvation, according to the life and teachings of Jesus the Liberator, has a political dimension and cannot be confined to questions of eternal life for individuals. But Schillebeeckx, as noted in Chapter 4, believes that the political dimension is but one—and not the only—additional dimension to the spiritual or existential. For Schillebeeckx, the divine gift of salvation which Jesus incarnated is not reducible to one or two dimensions of human experience; it is multidimensional. If salvation is to include humans and not just angels, it must be as multidimensional a reality as the human reality. Schillebeeckx shifts the discussion of authority away from revelation or dogma alone, toward the authority of Scripture, on the one hand, and the authority of experience, on the other. This move implies going beyond dogmatic interpretations of Scripture to historical-critical approaches, but also beyond the widespread assumption that "experience" means only subjective feelings to a more open, dialogical, relational notion of experience-and-interpretation. His multidimensional approach to understanding Jesus as Savior today most likely finds a ready audience with those (1) who accept his sense of disconnectedness between narrow ecclesiastical Christianity and the modern sense for the multidimensional character of human experience, and (2) who agree with him that for "salvation" to have any connection with experience (newly interpreted) it can no longer be so narrowly confined to the subject-object dualism of philosophers or to the otherworldly dualism and existentialism of much theology.

Lastly, Schillebeeckx, in his soteriologically based Christology, has yet to address the question of the salvific significance of other religions, but he, too, must ask how the salvation won in Jesus relates to other ways of salvation—lest he fall under Langdon Gilkey's justifiable criticism:

> No longer can any twentieth-century theologian either assume that truth and salvation do *not* exist outside of Christ or assume that he continue to avoid the issue as if it weren't there.[7]

Without necessarily endorsing Altizer's version of the universal Christ, Schillebeeckx's multidimensional view of experience and his sustained criticism of the "subject-object" split (that is, the assumption that subjective consciousness is a privileged observer or spectator of the objective world "out there") seem to prepare the way for something akin to Altizer's apocalyptic proposal. Altizer's notion is that salvation must begin with the destruction of the dualistic consciousness (the subject merely observing and using fellow creatures as objects). This destruction began when Jesus, by his parabolic utterance and actions, initiated universal consciousness. The final advent of that consciousness—already dawning in the postmodern period—cannot be described by any of us so long as we cling fiercely to our precious but deadly subjectivity.

Scholars and theologians of world religions might agree that if humans had a more universal consciousness it would be salvific indeed, but they are wary of supposing—as Altizer does—that such a salvific consciousness comes *only* by the words and actions of Jesus. If one dimension of the Christian experience of salvation is universal consciousness, then, surely, as a Christian I should be able to learn *something* about *that* dimension of salvation from those other faiths which do not encourage me to "cling" so fiercely to my subjectivity. In fact, to follow Jesus the Savior might imply that I should follow him into a deep immersion in other religions to the point of discovering there in them new and as yet undeveloped ways (which theological colleagues might regard as Buddhistic ways or Islamic ways or Hindu ways) for speaking of salvation.

This final, and as yet most uncharted, proposal for understanding the Christian way of salvation is gaining more and more appeal among those of us who find either that we can no longer tolerate the fugitive and cloistered, and therefore false, piety of the ecclesiastical ghetto, or that divine Providence (God's mysterious way of shaping and guiding the circumstances and events of our lives) is destroying our ghetto and forcing us out into the religiously pluralistic world of God's own making.

We have been asking how the various Christologies stand up under the *ultimate* norm or criterion: do they hinder and obscure, or do they clarify and communicate what must be done in order that the world be saved? If, as we have supposed, both lostness and salvation are multidimensional, it is no surprise that it takes many Christologies, that is, numerous theories, to do justice to the multifaceted fact. And it is no surprise that we can find much to appreciate in all the influential 20th-century theologians—from Barth to Altizer, from Pannenberg to Panikkar—for their real, if partial, success in expressing theologically (that is, in second-order theoretical terms) what people have in various ways experienced as fact.

Twentieth-century theology has produced a host of theological witnesses to Jesus. Because of the urgency of the times, a single witness may occasionally seem to silence or subdue all the others, at least in the short run. Barth's voice was such a one. But surely a great chorus of witnesses to the truth will always be preferable in the long run to a single voice. And each witness can and should be evaluated according to those secondary criteria which are appropriate to the context and to the audience being addressed. My argument has been that the ultimate worth of any interpretation of Jesus is how well or badly a Christology functions soteriologically. Even Barth was willing to have his Christology judged on those terms.[8]

Nevertheless, the collective wisdom of the churches may yet recognize that in the short term of special crisis or need the Christian mission and message in the 20th century and beyond are better served by an entire repertoire of interpretations than by only one of the various single-minded witnesses. The challenge for any Christian as pastor, preacher, missionary, citizen, and worker is to read the crisis in such a way that each of us can focus more effectively on God's saving work epitomized in Jesus either

- as the one who embodies the Word and thus saves us by calling us away from idolatry and transitory, dying systems;
- or as the one who reveals the Absolute Future and saves us from backward-looking hopelessness;
- or as the one who overcomes estrangement and saves us by returning us to our intended and essential unity with God;
- or as the one who incarnates the eternal, restless, and creative power of God, ceaselessly transforming the chaos of our misuse of freedom into a new creation;
- or as the one who draws us into solidarity with the oppressed, challenging those with power to revolutionize social structures by using that power to do justice, beginning with the poor;
- or as the one who by his suffering discloses how fractured are the many structures of human relatedness on which we are

totally dependent, but who also tenders to us God's forgiveness as the essential clue to how God wills to rule in the world;

- or as the one who by his words and actions releases a new apocalyptic consciousness, brings individualism to an end, begins the new age of universal humanity and thus both destroys and saves us;
- or as the one who waits for us among other religions and from their midst bids us leave the palaces of divisive, imperialistic Christendom and to join with our sisters and brothers in serving one another for the sake of the universal peace for which Jesus died.

Each of the theological witnesses in the representative list above must be judged at least partially successful in relating Jesus as Savior to a distinctive diagnosis of the human condition. In each case Jesus qualifies as the Christ in the sense of a modern equivalent of "Christ," but the various "Christs" can no more be easily harmonized than can the Christologies of the New Testament. Each of the modern equivalents tries to show that the "work" of salvation is truly and unsurpassably represented in Jesus, and that this work can be ultimately trusted because the "person" of Jesus Christ cannot be spoken of apart from God. The Word, The End, the New Being, the Principle of Creative Transformation, Liberator, and so forth, are modern cognates for "Christ"; that is, they are proposals for identifying Jesus and showing how Jesus, thus identified, corresponds to what God must do in order to save the world from unbelief or from hopelessness, estrangement, and all the other manifold dimensions of lostness.

It is simply inconceivable that Jesus of Nazareth would ever have been called "Messiah," "Anointed One," or "Christ" if no one had received him as the one sent by God to save them from sin and death, to reconcile them to God, and to assure them of the good news. The sheer facts that the first generation of Christians recorded for posterity his words, deeds, and death, and that they experienced his risen presence in the community as they celebrated the eucharistic banquet are testimony to the prior fact that he was experienced as good news from God. And the good news is this:

It is neither Caesar nor sin, it is neither death nor the devil, and it is not even God's own Law that ultimately rules creation, but it is

God who ultimately rules and the Way in which God rules in the world is Jesus.

Conversely, to contradict, deny, or oppose Jesus is to condemn oneself, or to be condemned (John 3:17f.), because in opposing Jesus one is opposing how God has willed to rule.

The Finality of Christ in the Postmodern Age

This book is a call to open up and enlarge the way we think about Jesus as Savior. It is not the first time in our history that Christians have had to change how we think about what we believe.

As in much theology today, there have been in these pages repeated references to the Enlightenment as the watershed which divided the history of Christianity into two parts: *before* the Enlightenment (that is, *traditional* Christianity, up to and including the Reformation recovery of Pauline and apocalyptic themes) and *after* the Enlightenment (*modern* Christianity's struggle to come to terms with historical consciousness, scientific worldviews, secular political systems, religious freedom, and autonomous philosophies). To some degree all "modern" theologians—fundamentalists might exclude themselves—believe it necessary to "demythologize" Christianity. That is, we all recognize that the thought-forms, language, imagery, symbols, and worldviews of the Scriptures and of the tradition prior to the Enlightenment have to be interpreted or translated into modern, i.e., post-Enlightenment idioms. "Modernity" itself, however, is but a transitory moment in history, and the signs are everywhere that "modern" is not only impossible to define satisfactorily but that the "Western" version of it (expressed primarily within European and North American social systems) has lost its potency as a model for other cultures to emulate. Many artists, writers, and educators in the West have themselves turned elsewhere for hope and inspiration; and many of the assumptions of post-Enlightenment modernity are more and more regarded with the same suspicion as certain assumptions of pre-Enlightenment Christianity. And so, without any clear idea of what is meant by the term (beyond the fairly general agreement that neither "modernity" nor any other "age" is the Golden Age) we now speak of this as the *postmodern* age.

Postmoderns share at least this much with apocalyptic times: we know it is genuinely possible that there will be no other age after this one. This could be the "last" age, not in the sense that no other age could conceivably be better than this, but in the sense that our predecessors of the previous age—the "moderns"—have bequeathed to our age the technical capacity to alter nature as no other age was able to do. The moderns educated and trained most of the powerful leaders of our time, instilling in them a shortsightedness, a narrowness of vision, and a mentality that make them prone to use their power to abuse nature and persons and thus to make life on earth for future generations impossible.

What we postmoderns do not share with certain apocalyptic interpretations of our time is a picture of God who as the omnipotent King will all by himself save us from our self-inflicted destruction by totally overwhelming human power. (The notion that God as almighty Ruler will cancel history like some dictatorial stage director and prevent a nuclear holocaust or an ecological disaster is totally incredible, scarcely biblical, and finally immoral, because it sanctifies inaction and lethargy. Even more incredible and unbiblical is the view that God will snatch or "rapture" true believers from destruction just in time.) Furthermore, many postmodern Christians seriously question the restricted notions of salvation common among *pre*-Enlightenment Christians, for example, of Luther's day, or *post*-Enlightenment Christians, for example, of Schleiermacher's or Kierkegaard's time, namely, that justification by faith or forgiveness of sins is the only salvation that matters. Such personalistic notions of salvation were obviously meaningful for Christians on both sides of the Enlightenment watershed; they were reenforced by mythic images of God as the all-powerful King, with Jesus as the King's Son sent to do his Father's bidding and to gain release, forgiveness, and pardon for the King's subjects. But that personalistic and royal imagery is no longer easily accepted, and it is positively of no help in reinterpreting what Jesus and salvation can mean for the postmodern age.

Terms like God as Omnipotent Ruler, kingdom of God, Jesus as Lord, and many others, assume a picture of reality which is difficult if not impossible for Christians in the postmodern age. Except for those who have been brought up in a sectarian ghetto, how we think and our various conceptions of reality do not assume the traditional picture of reality, because we have been shaped by very different circumstances. For example, as postmoderns we do not derive our notions of power and authority from divinely ordained kings, but from experiences of authority as shared, earned, and therefore relative. And our pictures of the world and the world's causal connections are influenced by events of the space age, the nuclear age, the age of global interdependence. For postmoderns, "salvation" must include social strategies for preventing ecological disaster, nuclear holocaust, and oppression of the poor, and cannot be restricted to the imagery of interpersonal transactions between the Absolute King and his disobedient subjects, even though that imagery has honored place in the Bible and in the prayers and hymnody of the church.

The biblical and traditional conceptions of sin and salvation reflect ancient political and social arrangements (hierarchical kingdoms and patriarchal families) which are alien to us, which few of us would want to return to, and which need no longer exercise such control over the way we *think* about sin and salvation and therefore think of Jesus as Savior. I agree with Gordon Kaufman of Harvard:

> The conception of sin as primarily a kind of personal disobedience or violation of the divine will, and salvation as being rescued from that condition of alienation and guilt, is rooted almost completely in the mythic picture which presents God as a divine king and father, and our relationship to God as the interpersonal and political one of subjects and children.[9]

There is no doubt that the personalistic imagery so favored in the Bible and in the Reformation tradition has been religiously effective. Kaufman's complaint is that the religious dimension is too often isolated from the other dimensions of life which are also threatened by lostness: the political, economic, cultural, and the biological, as well as the ecological and historical interconnections without which there could be no life. Clergy and theologians, who can be said to have a vested interest in the "religious" (understood as the inner

and personal) dimension, tend to think that the other dimensions
have nothing to do with salvation. Kaufman writes:

> The problem of salvation is the problem of finding a way to keep all
> the diverse, complexly interdependent dimensions of life in harmo-
> nious balance and development. . . . [In addition to experts in reli-
> gious traditions it] requires also the combined expertise and efforts
> of psychologists and chemists, engineers and artists, politicians and
> farmers, educators, physicians, labourers and many others. . . . Sal-
> vation should no longer be conceived as a singular process or activity,
> a unilateral action from on high coming down to earth and working
> primarily in and through the church.[10]

At this point the nervous question arises, "If we redefine salvation
and Jesus' person and work so broadly, what is left of the claims
for the finality and the distinctiveness of Christianity?"

I have emphasized that all theological claims for the truth of
Christianity arose as the inevitable consequence of reflecting or theorizing on the experience of Jesus as Savior. The fact that Jesus was
so experienced lies behind the New Testament and behind its testimonies to Jesus as Christ, as Lord, as Son of God, or as the Word
made flesh. The fact that Jesus is still so experienced is one of the
facts which accounts for the continuation of the Christian movement.
But memories of past experiences alone do not guarantee the continuation of the Christian movement any more than a nation or a
marriage can survive on memories alone; to survive, the Christian
movement must have sound teaching and clear doctrine in order to
protect, clarify, and communicate all that is implied by the experienced fact of Jesus as Savior. Remember that all facts are theory-
dependent. Even the facts upon which the salvation of the world
hangs cannot be protected, clarified, or communicated without sound
teaching, adequate theories, or clear doctrine.

Christianity is a historical movement, and not a docetic one float-
ing above or outside history; it depends on doctrine for its continuation. Sound doctrine is absolutely necessary for the church, but
no doctrine is in itself absolute; doctrines also are historical. Virtually all theologians agree that doctrines are like ideas—they developed historically. Even the guidance of the Spirit does not eliminate social, cultural, and historical factors. But when the absolute

necessity for "sound" teaching or "pure" doctrine is taken to mean doctrine that is itself finished, beyond change, fixed for all time, absolute and eternal, then, unfortunately, instead of pointing to the genuine, historical occasions of salvation, no matter where they happen, or instead of participating in or being channels of the reality of salvation, doctrine points to itself as the absolute test for determining *who is saved,* usually meaning whoever believes the doctrine. The all-too-familiar end result is that salvation is held captive to "religion" alone, and the dispensation of salvation is presided over by clergy and theologians of "pure doctrine," who in the name of protecting the "finality" of Christianity place limits on the generosity of God or the scope of God's saving activity.

The concern for sound doctrine is especially hazardous in the postmodern world. The radical openness and frightening contingency of "the postmodern age" includes the genuine possibility of man-made catastrophe in the near future. Most of the narrow, closed, or restricted programs for saving us—i.e., many of the religious and ideological "isms" which bid for our loyalty and which carry out their sometimes ruthless crusades—propose to save us by shutting down all other options so that, in practice, instead of saving us from catastrophe they intensify the likelihood of it. Concern for the integrity and soundness of doctrine about the "finality" of Christ can and often does (but need not) propel Christians into transforming their belief in Jesus as Savior into one more dangerous fanaticism.

The Anonymous Christ

This study of 20th-century Christology cannot conclude without a brief discussion of why it is still essential for the church not only to win the *total commitment* of others to Jesus as Savior but also to encourage *total openness* to the multiplying dimensions of salvation in this postmodern age. This discussion has two parts.

1. The history and theology of Jesus

The postmodern age does not eliminate beliefs; rather, the urgency of beliefs is all the greater. The facts of life in the postmodern age are radical openness, radical contingency, and the genuine possibility of unspeakable catastrophe to the human race in the near future.

Anyone could conceivably respond to those facts of life by believing and so acting as though what *can* go wrong *will* go wrong, and if a sufficient number of others so believe and act, the belief itself becomes one of the actual causes of what goes wrong. Contingency means that the future is vulnerable to what we believe (i.e., "what can go wrong" simply assumes the *fact* that much *can* go wrong, and "will go wrong" states a *belief* which, when acted upon, is one of the actual causes of what *will* happen as loss). All of this speaks for the importance of remembering the history and telling the story of Jesus.

The history of Jesus is crucial historical evidence that even in a world where things can go wrong, salvation can also happen. In the history of Jesus salvation took many forms: the sick were healed, the lepers were cleansed, the hungry were fed, captives were released, and the poor had good news preached to them. Such events aroused opposition: John the Baptizer, who first announced the advent of Jesus, was beheaded; Jesus was publicly executed. Those who believed Jesus to be good news from God were shocked to discover that his death did not end it all. For a few weeks they experienced him alive among them, and when those experiences ended they were given new life in the Spirit of God who had sent Jesus. That New Testament history of Jesus, which has guided the lives of Christians since then and which is inseparable from those who have believed in him, is—as history—evidence against the contrary belief that what can go wrong inevitably will go wrong. In this postmodern age much is at stake in remembering and telling that history.

Because of that history a *theology* developed and, while the theology is distinguishable from the history of Jesus, it is not finally separable from that history. The theology continues to develop even today; hence this and many other books continue to be written. The theology especially centers on the apostles' testimony concerning the relation of Jesus to God who is spoken of in the Hebrew Scriptures. The apostolic testimony to that relationship carries with it a claim for the universal and everlasting significance of what happened in the history of Jesus. In other words, while the *history* of Jesus is evidence against the contrary belief that what can go wrong will go wrong, the *theology* of Jesus as the Christ is an invitation to apply it to everything in all of creation, beginning with oneself and radiating out to the whole cosmos (e.g., Rom. 8:31ff.; Col. 1:15ff.). The history of Jesus—this theology claims—was not a fluke, nor an accident, nor a one-in-a-trillion chance but rather—even in a world where everything *can* go wrong and still *might* go horribly wrong very soon—an invitation to believe that the way the entire world is put together, the very principle of its life and operation, supports what happened in Jesus; in traditional language, it was willed by God. The evidence is that Jesus was experienced as Savior; that is a *fact* of history. It is a matter of *faith,* says this Christian *theology,* whether you or I believe that what happened in Jesus continues to be effective, active, and savingly at work in all of creation and in all of history as God's way of ruling the world. That faith is absolutely crucial for the salvation of the world.

And so, in a postmodern age the *history* of Jesus is simply one piece of indispensable evidence against the belief that what can go wrong will go wrong, an erroneous belief which, if it were to spread even further, could doom the world. Again and again, cynical people have had to qualify their own bitter and negative view of the world when faced with the evidence of lives influenced by the history of Jesus. Every such empirical challenge to cynicism has salvific effect for the postmodern age, because it reduces the odds that negative beliefs will very soon cause world disaster.

The *theology* of Jesus as Savior is also simply indispensable for communicating an invitation to all people. Because the future really is vulnerable to belief, the salvation of the world is dependent on all nations believing that the world—i.e., reality—is not "rigged" against the survival of humanity, nor that it is merely a matter of odds which cannot be significantly altered. The *theology* (Who was Jesus? What is salvation?) of Jesus as Savior proposes that what happened in Jesus is not an isolated chance event, that the history of Jesus was also God's history, that this saving event was supported by the One whose presence and power uphold all creation, that God wills all nations to live in universal harmony and peace, that God can be trusted to be impartial and not to go back on God's Word made visible in Jesus.

It is the peculiar work of theology to defend, to clarify, and ultimately to make the case: that Jesus is Savior; that what happened in the local history of Jesus, beginning in the New Testament, is what God did for the salvation of the world; that the God who wills to save the world is everywhere and always present in the world. It is for the sake of the world's salvation that theology tries so to speak of God's work in Jesus that all people can believe in him as Savior. The evidence against the case which theology tries to make abounds: widespread ignorance of the Jesus story, demonic resistance to the total well-being of all creatures, preoccupation with self, tribe, nation, and religion. The theological task is to make clear that God has given us a literally unsurpassable reason for believing that salvation for all is still a real possibility—in spite of these factors. The theological case rests on this: *that Jesus is the best and final evidence that not even God can do more than die at the hands of those who reject the offer of salvation.* On the level of human history there is nothing "more" that could possibly demonstrate just how determined God is to win the trust of all nations.

The *theological* task, then, is to show that what happened in Jesus is God's "final" offer, not in the petulant commercial sense of "take it or leave it," but in the sense that even God has nothing more to offer for the salvation of humanity. This is the limit of what is historically possible for God. Jesus is the "only" Son of God because in him God exhausted the limits, limits which God has set for the sake of "getting through" to the world. If that sacrifice does not break and win the stubborn hearts of human beings, neither would another child, or another, or still another.

Why try to win the *total commitment* of others to Jesus as Savior? On this reading, it is not because Christianity is morally or intellectually superior to other religions (it is not) nor that Christianity should be so exclusively "number one" in everybody's allegiance that no criticism from without be heard (it should not), nor even because Christianity will save them (it will not). The missionary motive for winning commitment to Jesus as Savior is finally based on *God's* commitment to the salvation of the world. To tell others the scriptural story of Jesus is to inform them of the ultimate demonstration of God's love for humanity. Half-hearted commitment to telling that story is to be half-hearted about the future, the destiny— in short, the salvation—of the world.

2. The anonymity of Christ

It is important not to confuse the term "the anonymous Christ" with Rahner's famous one, "the anonymous Christian." An anonymous Christian could only be a person who has learned the history of Jesus and who believes that the history of Jesus and God's history of salvation coincide, but then tells no one about that commitment. Such a "Christian" betrays the faith, indeed is no Christian at all. To be Christian is to be public about one's commitment and to be steadfast in that commitment. *The Anonymous Christ* does not propose that one can be a Christian and not know it, or that one can be a Christian and be intentionally secretive about it. Rather, it is a term which proposes that Christians, while firm in *their* commitment to Jesus as the final demonstration of *God's* commitment to the salvation of the world, are also obliged to be open to the multiplying dimensions and occasions where salvation actually happens in the world.

All of this means that when Christians use terms like "only Son" or "no other name" the exclusivity is strictly "theological" in the sense that God literally could do no more than (i.e., God limited Godself to) what God has done in Jesus. Nothing more, nothing greater, could be done even by God to win the faith, and therefore the salvation, of humanity—and still be God's act. Jesus as "limit" defines God as the God who is self-determined to love the world, and thus all of God's actions are limited to the bounds of that self-determination. Put differently, Jesus is the "final" demonstration that God's actions are determined by love, that in him God has exhausted the limits of love and when that love-to-the-limit was cruelly rejected, it did not "crack" or weaken God's own determination to stay within the limit. The exclusiveness refers to *God* having determined to exclude other possibilities for Godself, and Jesus is the unsurpassable historical instance of that self-limitation.

Rahner's term "the anonymous Christian" purports to celebrate the inclusiveness of the love of God from which no one is excluded, but it misleads because it misses what is claimed for the history of Jesus, namely, that *in Jesus God has excluded for God's own self— and for all religions as well—certain alternative ways of salvation.* God does not place limits on who is or can be saved or under the auspices of which religion or nonreligion salvation does or can occur.

God alone saves by placing limits on God. This does *not* imply that God has limited salvation to Christians only, thereby excluding *all* other ways; it does imply that the saving will of God excludes *those* ways which, in the name of religion or in the name of nation or even in the name of Christ, do to others what was done to Jesus. The cross of Christ is God's way of showing the limits beyond which God cannot go for the salvation of the world, and at the same time the cross slams the door on any religion or social system which tries to use coercive methods—mental, physical, spiritual, or otherwise— as final means for saving the world. Some ways—even some "Christian" ways—*are* excluded by God's way, which Christian theology discerns as the history of Jesus. *How* God acts in the world, then, is "finally" defined by God's limitation: when Jesus died he said, "It is finished."

But *where* and *when* and under *whose* "religious" or nonreligious auspices God acts savingly in the world are questions not settled by the history of Jesus, a history which theologically *does exclude some ways* but excludes *no* place, *no* time, *no* circumstances, *no* culture, and *no* religious tradition. There is no historical or convincing theological reason for excluding any place, time, circumstance, culture, or religious tradition as the occasion for God's way of acting savingly. Christians, of course, know the Christ in and as the history of Jesus, and it is in his history that one can know not only *how* God has acted and acts savingly but also—in the case of Jesus— the specifics of where and when and in what circumstances. But when that history alone dominates our thinking about salvation, whether as biblicism, confessionalism, orthodoxism, or whatever, the resulting Christologies are *more* exclusive than God!

The principal theological matter that is settled or made final (that is, finished) by the history which Jesus carried out in Palestine is that in Jesus God determined that no *other* way of acting savingly in the world than this way (which led to the cross) can be called God's way of acting savingly. *Jesus constitutes what God has willed to be God's way of saving the world.* But, since God is necessarily present and active everywhere and not just in first-century Palestine, the local history of Jesus cannot be the limit or the final determination of where and when and under whose auspices God is also savingly active as the one who can only be called the Anonymous Christ.

The *how* of God's saving power is finally, definitively, and unsurpassably given in Jesus of Nazareth. But that very local historical definition of the "power that saves" can also be found in many exemplifications, and in the multiple dimensions of salvation. This book has documented how, as an aggregate, 20th-century theologians have expanded the notion of the power that saves to include a variety of Christologies. Surely, Christians can also learn to honor "the Anonymous Christ." That term is used here in several senses.

First, in an art gallery I might gaze upon, or contemplate, or enter into, or enjoy, or be engulfed by, or be puzzled by, a painting. It is undeniable that the painting is there for me. This gift is provided for me. I notice that the donor is "anonymous." The power of the gift to enrich me or to influence me is not diminished merely because I do not know the giver. I surely enjoy the benefits of the gift. I do not give those benefits to myself, for without the gift from the anonymous donor I could not know or enjoy what comes to me through the agency of the generous giver. I also surely know something of the anonymous donor's will and intention. I do not lack the benefit which the giver has intended for me. "To know Christ is to know his benefits" at least means that something of the generosity and grace of Christ is known through the experience of salvation.

"The power that saves" may be like trying to define art. Most of us are probably so unsure of what art is that we would scarcely risk buying or displaying a painting that is unsigned, or done by an unknown artist, or whose previous owner was not a well-known collector. It is only when the signature is authenticated that we readily appreciate what we are seeing. Someone whispers, "Picasso, you know," or "It was owned by the Rockefellers," and we then feel safe in enjoying what is given us to behold.

The term *anonymous* also hints strongly of the mysterious and the ominous, and thus is quite properly applied to the Christ. It reminds us that we do not grasp the entirety of God's saving work in the world through the personal or local or familiar experiences of salvation, no matter how extraordinary its benefits. "To know Christ is to know his benefits"—indeed, but it is not to know the Christ fully. The proposal that Christians are able to speak of the Anonymous Christ is perhaps a bold one, but the boldness is warranted by the recognition that while Jesus is the final norm for speaking of the Christ, no Christology nor any experience of salvation is exhaustive of the reality of Christ. Likewise, God's saving work, which was given its final expression in Jesus, can never be confined to or controlled by biblical scholarship's reconstruction of the redemptive event centering on Jesus of Nazareth. As one proposal for designating Jesus as God's way of working redemptively in the world, the Anonymous Christ cautions all believers and their theologians that God's ways are ubiquitous and hidden, and therefore somewhat elusive. The Anonymous Christ is a reminder that our Christologies are always relative, time-bound, and potential instruments for betraying Christ. Christologies can witness to the reality of Christ, but the reality always eludes capture by Christology.

The Anonymous Christ, then, de-familiarizes in the sense that it questions easy acceptance of all that is too familiar or allegedly final about Christological formulations. The term also is an invitation to adventure and exploration into the unfamiliar where we do not ordinarily expect to find the Christ, namely, the many dimensions of human experience, achievement, and failure where Jesus is not yet named. *Anonymous* speaks of the vague as well as the ominous and the hidden, but the term is not hopelessly vague, because it represents a promise, a challenge, an invitation, a call that we go forward into those places where Christ is not yet named as Jesus but where Christ is only and nothing more than the Anonymous Christ.

Christians are those who know the history of Jesus as the final definition of the power that saves, but today lack a Christology ample enough to discern the multiplying dimensions of salvation in the postmodern age. Many times our confidence in the grace of God is so shaky and limited that we feel we cannot call a deed or a project or a task "salvific" unless it is clearly given under the auspices of a Christian agency or enacted quite explicitly in the name of Jesus. This means that the history of Jesus, while it is for *Christians* the history which defines the way of salvation, nevertheless can open *anyone* to recognize the power that saves even where there is no "signature."

To believe in Jesus as Savior is to believe that in him God has defined salvation once for all. Therefore some ways of salvation are excluded, even some ways endorsed by churches. It is God who has determined to *save* the world and has determined *how* the world is to be saved. That way is disclosed in Jesus. This does not mean that salvation happens only through the mission of the church, but it does mean that all ways of salvation are judged by God's ultimate determination: salvation is not through the power of Caesar nor through trappings of religion but through Jesus as God's way of living and ruling in the world. That way includes suffering and death, but that way is also vindicated by the resurrection.

The very logic of the Christian witness to Jesus as Savior is exclusive. Some ways of salvation are excluded. But Christ is not excluded from any of God's salvific actions in the world. Christians are bold to speak of Jesus as the final way of salvation, but such speaking is not warrant for claiming finality for any one Christology. This study has proposed a certain modesty in speaking of the Christ—to speak of Christ as the Anonymous Christ who is revealed in Jesus but also hidden in God's saving actions. Today there are many pragmatic (i.e., open to change) strategies for making partial but verifiable gains in furthering the truth, restoring order, overcoming ignorance, fighting oppression, establishing freedom, increasing justice, nurturing beauty, protecting the environment, strengthening the vulnerable, healing the sick, feeding the hungry, reconciling enemies, comforting the bereaved, reducing violence, protesting torture, and welcoming strangers. It is not yet too late for the Anonymous Christ to call Christians in this postmodern age to participate in all such ministries through which God's saving purpose is realized in the world.

NOTES

Chapter One: The Many Dimensions of Lostness

1. Panikkar writes, "In spite of the scores of attempts at defining religion I may venture this simple and brief statement: Religion is the path Man follows in order to reach the purpose of life, or, shorter, religion is the *way of salvation*. One has to add immediately that here the words 'way' and 'salvation' do not claim any specific content; rather they stand for the existential pilgrimage Man undertakes in the belief that this enterprise will help him achieve the final purpose or end of life. . . . In other words, under the particular perspective that we may call religion, every human culture presents three elements: (1) a vision of Man as he actually appears to be . . . (2) a certain more or less developed notion of the end or final station of Man . . . and (3) the means for going from the former situation to the the latter" (R. Panikkar, *The Intra-Religious Dialogue* [New York: Paulist, 1978], p. 78).

2. The word *paradidonai* is even more richly nuanced in the New Testament usage where its connection with soteriological themes is unmistakable. The following analysis is instructive: "A basic element in the passion predictions is their use of the verb *paradidonai*, which is fundamental to both the second and third predictions [in Mark] ('The Son of Man will be delivered into. . . ,' 10:32; 'The Son of Man will be delivered to . . .') This use of Son of Man with *paradinonai* in connection with the passion of Jesus is a well marked tradition in the early church. It begins in a purely descriptive use, describing the passion of Jesus in accordance with a usage established in Jewish literature in connection with the fate of the prophets. In this sense we find the use of the verb in the passion narrative (Mark 15:1, 10, 15, 35) and in the stylized representation of Judas (Matthew 10:4 and frequently). The specifically Christian use begins in early Christian passion apologetic where it is used with the Son of Man to stress the divine necessity for the passion. . . . From this apologetic use there developed a soteriological use. . ." (Norman Perrin in *Christology and A Modern Pilgrimage,* ed. Hans Dieter Betz [Claremont, 1971], pp. 23f.).

3. Schubert Ogden, in *The Point of Christology* (San Francisco: Harper and Row, 1982), has argued that modern Christologies have put the wrong question to

the New Testament witnesses. The approach in these pages is, in the main, in agreement with his criticism. The starting point for Christology, indeed the *point* of Christology, is to show how Jesus is Savior. In Ogden's terminology it is to show how Jesus is the answer to the complex question of the meaning of existence, which question can be phrased, "Whom can I trust?" or "Who am I?" or "How am I to live?" See my review in *Currents in Contemporary Christology* (AAR Newsletter, III, no. 3), pp. 6-13.

4. David Tracy, *Blessed Rage for Order* (New York: Seabury, 1975), p. 4.

5. Cf. Peter Berger, *The Sacred Canopy: Elements of a Sociological Theory of Religion* (New York: Doubleday, 1967).

6. Emil Brunner, in the following passage, risks actually denying that Jesus was at all an historical figure (tantamount to betraying him whom he would defend against historicist criticism): "It is of the essence of the Christian faith that its relation to history should be entirely different from that of any other religion or philosophy. In the ordinary sense of the word it is not concerned with history at all. It is what it is through its relation to that unique event, which, although it is a fact of history, does not gain its unique character from its historical connection. It is this which determines the peculiar relation of the Christian faith to history in general. To the Christian faith revelation does not mean a reverent process of tracing the ways of God in history . . . . But precisely because something superhistorical, unique, absolutely decisive has entered into human history, to faith history means something different from its meaning for all other forms of thought" (p. 153). "The Atonement is not history. The Atonement . . . is not anything that can be perceived from the point of view of history. This event does not belong to the historical plane. It is super-history; it lies in the dimension which no historian can know in so far as he is merely an historian" (p. 504). These sentences are from Emil Brunner, *The Mediator* (Philadelphia: Westminster, 1947; first published in 1927.) For at least one generation of theological students in America, Brunner's work was standard fare. He was a very influential neoorthodox theologian in America and elsewhere in the 1940s and 1950s; probably more American clergy imbibed their neoorthodoxy from Brunner than from Barth.

7. The work of Rosemary Radford Ruether has been especially effective in making this point. See her *Faith and Fratricide* (New York: Seabury, 1974) and *To Change the World* (New York: Crossroad, 1981). The literature exposing the ideological (mis)use of Christology multiplies annually.

8. Cf. Hans Conzelmann, *Jesus* (Philadelphia: Fortress, 1973), pp. 36-50.

9. See Martin Hengel, *The Atonement: The Origins of the Doctrine in the New Testament* (Philadelphia: Fortress, 1981): "If Jesus had no messianic features at all, the origins of the Christian kerygma would remain completely inexplicable and mysterious" (p. 48). See also Hengel, *The Son of God* (Philadelphia: Fortress, 1976): The early communities assumed that the experienced fact of Jesus as Savior was "an episode in salvation history" but right from the beginning they were at pains to interpret *this* episode in terms of a consistent Christology so that Jesus was not one episode only but the "fulfiller of the promise of the old covenant, the sole mediator of salvation . . ." (pp. 90f.). For a summary of the several New Testament Christologies see R. H. Fuller and Pheme Perkins, *Who Is This Christ?* (Philadelphia: Fortress, 1983). See

also James D. G. Dunn, *Christology in the Making* (Philadelphia: Westminster, 1980), pp. 265-267, where he summarizes New Testament scholarship on the question of multiple Christologies. He writes, "Christology should not be narrowly confined to one particular assessment of Christ nor should it play off one against another nor should it insist on squeezing all the different NT conceptualizations into one particular 'shape', but it should recognize that from the first the significance of Christ could only be apprehended by a diversity of formulations, which, though not always strictly compatible with each other, were not regarded as rendering each other invalid." Finally, E. P. Sanders argues at great length that Jesus' work "is not to be understood as one of polar opposition between a good will [Jesus] and men of bad intent [Jews]," that Jesus' work is best understood in the context of Jewish "restoration eschatology," and that Jesus spent his time "preparing his followers and hearers for the coming redemption . . ." (*Jesus and Judaism* [Philadelphia: Fortress, 1985], pp. 333-339).

10. While every theologian acknowledges that Christology presupposes soteriology, most theologians do not begin their expositions with soteriology but with Christology. Consider, e.g., Paul Tillich, *Systematic Theology*, vol. 2 (Chicago, University of Chicago Press, 1957): "The early church was well aware that christology is an existentially necessary, though not a theoretically interesting, work of the church. Its ultimate criterion, therefore, is existential itself. It is soteriological" (p. 146). There are good and sound reasons for that strategy. Even though it is a truism that no one has ever been saved by either a "high" or a "low" Christology, the essential claims for the truth of salvation can be and often have been obscured or even denied by a faulty Christology. Historians are agreed that what was at stake in the theological battles leading up to the Council of Chalcedon was nothing less than what was implied when Christians claim that Jesus is Savior. See for example, Jaroslav Pelikan, *The Emergence of the Catholic Tradition, 100–600*, The Christian Tradition: A History of the Development of Doctrine, vol. 1, (Chicago: University of Chicago, 1971): "Amid the varieties of metaphors in which they conceived the meaning of salvation, all Christians shared the conviction that salvation was the work of no being less than the Lord of heaven and earth . . . . Christians were sure that the Redeemer did not belong to some lower order of divine reality but was God himself" (p. 145). A very brief and readable survey of the history can be found in George H. Tavard, *Images of Christ: An Inquiry into Christology* (Washington: University Press of America, 1982). This primer highlights the major issues of each period of the church's reflections on Christ. Tavard's own bias is for the patristic period as normative.

Conzelmann points out that salvation was the content of Jesus' teaching, but not in any sense that can be detached from the teacher. "The connection of salvation with the person of Jesus lies simply in the fact that *he* offers this salvation as present, final possibility, that he now comforts the poor, and calls sinners to himself. . . . The form of Jesus' teaching corresponds to the content. Jesus does not summon people to an objective consideration of God, the world, and man, but grasps the hearer directly and reveals his situation through beatitudes (*makarismos*), the prophetic call, threats (Drohwort), through illumination in the style of wisdom, through his parables. Even his interpretation of scripture is not that of a detached observer, but is 'actualizing' " (*Jesus,* pp. 51f.). Eduard Schweizer, in a similar vein, speaks of Jesus as the man who fits no formula and who refuses titles or definitions: "By this very act of avoiding all common labels, Jesus helps free the heart of the man who encounters him. He wants to enter into this heart himself, in all the reality of what he does and says, not as an image already formed before he himself has a chance to encounter that person" (*Jesus* [Richmond: John Knox, 1971], p. 22).

Finally, Wolfhart Pannenberg, in *Jesus—God and Man* (Philadelphia: Westminster, 1968), acknowledges that in the history of Christianity "almost all christological conceptions have had soteriological motifs. Changes in the soteriological interest . . . explain, at least in part, the different forms christology has taken at different times" (p. 39). But Pannenberg rejects this approach to Christology because he suspects that it will involve "projections on Jesus' figure the human desire for salvation" (p. 47). Apparently, this method is too relativistic or subjectivistic for Pannenberg and so he sets out to establish a way to demonstrate the relationship between Jesus and God independently of any soteriological bias. A later chapter will suggest that Pannenberg's method itself is based on a perception of the human predicament, namely, the problem of knowledge. Instead of himself being innocent of some "projection," Pannenberg also approaches Jesus with a soteriological question: How can Jesus save from the ambiguities of history which relativize all human knowing?

11. The question is fundamentally an anxious one: How can faith as utter dependence or trust rest upon anything that is relative and ambiguous? Ernst Troeltsch set the terms of the argument for the 20th century in *The Absoluteness of Christianity and the History of Religion* (London: SCM, 1971; first published in 1901). Perhaps the best discussion of the problem is that of Van A. Harvey, *The Historian and the Believer* (New York: Macmillan, 1966).

12. Langdon Gilkey's analysis of the plight of the historically conscious believer has become a standard reference which nearly 25 years ago established the basic terms of the discussion. See "Cosmology, Ontology and the Travail of Biblical Language," *Journal of Religion* 41 (1962):194-205.

13. Theological proposals for the ideal way to read the Scriptures abound. One important account of these is David Kelsey's *The Uses of Scripture in Modern Theology* (Philadelphia: Fortress, 1975).

14. The urgent summons to revise our interpretations of Jesus has been issued by numerous authors. Three are especially striking: Elizabeth Schussler Fiorenza, *In Memory of Her: A Feminist Theological Reconstruction of Christian Origins* (New York: Crossroad, 1983); Eugene B. Borowitz, *Contemporary Christologies: A Jewish Response* (New York: Paulist, 1980); and Charlotte Klein, *Anti-Judaism in Christian Theology* (Philadelphia: Fortress, 1978).

15. There are major exceptions to this statement. Gustaf Aulen's critical survey of the ways in which the church interpreted Christ as the one who atones for sin was an important contribution: *Christus Victor: An Historical Study of the Three Main Types of the Idea of Atonement* (New York: Macmillan, 1951). About the same time, Shailer Mathews surveyed the history of the doctrine of atonement and noted a certain progression of atonement views, each of which he then correlated with presuppositions about the social order which prevailed at

the time. Unlike Aulen, Mathews makes no judgments about which of the successive patterns is normative (*The Atonement and the Social Process* [New York: Macmillan, 1930]). More recently, F. W. Dillistone has arranged views on the atonement according to literary categories and, unlike Mathews, does not propose a reinterpretation of atonement in evolutionary and social terms that will be coherent to the modern mind. For Dillistone, views of atonement gain whatever power they have from analogies and parables which are not essentially weakened by changing worldviews (*The Christian Understanding of Atonement* [Philadelphia Westminster, 1968]). George Rupp's *Christologies and Cultures: Toward a Typology of Religious Worldviews* (Paris: Mouton, 1974) is a successor more of Mathews' approach. He analyzes atonement theories according to two sets of variables: realist/nominalist and transactional/processive. He develops an argument for a realist/nominalist/processive criterion for assessing the viability of any Christology in a culturally pluralistic age.

16. I hope that the phrase "the experienced fact of Jesus as Savior" will become clear as it is encountered in this essay. The reader should be advised, however, that the word *fact* here is deliberately chosen and then amplified by the qualifiers surrounding it to be an inclusive term. Thus, those meanings of "fact" which presume either an exclusive "objectivity" or exclusive "relativity" or "subjectivity" are set aside. The approach here would, in some circles, be called postmodern in the sense that "modern" is intended to refer to the assumption of an absolute and unbridgeable split between two forms of "knowledge" where in one category are fact, objectivity, reason, the sciences, the provable, and humans as physically conditioned and empiricism. In the other are value, subjectivity, faith (i.e., prejudice), mere opinion, the humanities, mere assertion, the unprovable notions of "self," "mind," etc., and idealism. See Wayne Booth, *Modern Dogma and the Rhetoric of Assent* (Chicago: University of Chicago Press, 1974) for a readable and persuasive argument for a postmodernist view of what counts as knowledge and fact.

Professor George Lindbeck seems to accept the modernist dogma which splits subject and object, value and fact, inner and outer. For him "experience" is only inner, private, and prelinguistic and thus cannot be the basis for understanding innovation in a religious tradition. Religious innovation comes from the *outside*, when one religious tradition encounters a new situation and cannot accommodate the anomalies. "Religious changes or innovation must be understood not as proceeding from new experiences, but as resulting from the interactions of a cultural-linguistic system with changing situations." Presumably, then, Christianity arose not because Jesus was experienced as Savior but "because a religious interpretive scheme"—the Jewish tradition—had developed "anomalies in its application in new contexts" and Jesus was a figure who discovered "the concepts that remove the anomalies." See *The Nature of Doctrine, Religion and Theology in a Postliberal Age* (Philadelphia: Westminster, 1984), p. 39.

17. It should be apparent, then, that any "search for the historical Jesus" which *begins* with the notion of "historical" as nonrelative, nonsocial, nonambiguous, independent of prior perceptions or theories, and stripped of all valuational language, is simply impossible. The historical Jesus is the only kind of historical

figure that is conceivable or knowable—namely, the Jesus-as-Jesus-was-experienced. Jesus-as-experienced will include the testimony of believers and nonbelievers alike. Any recovery of the historical Jesus in that sense, then, will be very complex, but surely not impossible. On the other hand, a new historicism which goes beyond objectivism and relativism will call for new interpretation. For one suggestion of such a hermeneutical proposal, see Richard J. Bernstein, *Beyond Objectivism and Relativism: Science, Hermeneutics and Praxis* (Philadelphia: University of Pennsylvania Press, 1983). See also Norman Perrin, "Jesus and the Theology of the New Testament," *Journal of Religion* 64 (1984): 419, "The Jesus of the New Testament is the Jesus of Christian faith; he is the Jesus of the faith or perspectival image of Christian experience. . . . I must begin where this New Testament begins, with the Jesus Christ who is always the Jesus of Christian experience, a blend of the Jesus who was and of the Christ who is" (p. 419).

18. This is certainly Schillebeeckx's argument, as will be more apparent in a later chapter, but it has also been stated by those scholars already cited: Conzelmann, Hengel, Fuller, Schweizer, and Sanders. Any inferences which might be drawn about Jesus *in se*—his mind, his intention, his self-understanding—can only be inferences, but are not irrational for being so. Indeed, they would be necessary, but not sufficient, for any credible exposition. Schillebeeckx, as will be noted later, finds it quite legitimate to infer from New Testament sources certain clear features of Jesus' self-understanding which one can deny only by rejecting the historical character of the New Testament.

19. Apart from this historical and epistemological point, there is another. Far too much weight may have been placed on the resurrection and exaltation of the crucified Jesus. Both Hengel and Nils Dahl seem to be in agreement that "resurrection and exaltation could not by themselves serve as a justification for holding Jesus to be Messiah" (cf. Hengel, *The Atonement*, p. 41; also N. A. Dahl, *The Crucified Messiah* [Minneapolis: Augsburg, 1974]).

20. The reader is reminded that the truth claims implied by the facts being pointed to here have not yet been investigated, which investigation is the proper task of soteriology and Christology. The facts as stated are complex and they bristle with valuational content, but whatever truth may be implied has not been made explicit by the mere report of the facts. It is a fact that a majority of Americans voting in 1984 believed Ronald Reagan to be the better candidate for president but as a fact this does not necessarily imply that the majority voted for what was best or truthful about the United States in the 1980s. What is true is that the New Testament could not have been written without facts (1) and (2). Indeed, apart from such facts—which, of course, include faith—there would have been little of what we call the New Testament. Norman Perrin writes, "From the very beginning the synoptic tradition was a-historical, if by historical one means to imply a concern for Jesus 'as he actually was' " *(Christology and A Modern Pilgrimage,* p. 68).

21. None of the early creeds "specified in any detail how the salvation which was the purpose of Christ's coming was related to [the] events in his earthly and heavenly states . . . . The saving work of Christ remained dogmatically undefined. Yet it was certainly a major constituent of Christian doctrine . . ." (Pelikan, *The Emergence*, pp. 141f.).

22. The experienced fact of Jesus as Savior, in short, required something *like* a dogma of the two natures of Christ. The "hardening" is not traceable to this formal requirement *that* there be a dogma but to the tendency to define the divine nature as invulnerable to suffering and absolutely beyond change, and to define human nature as incapable of anything divine because of the radicality of sin. Divine and human are thus thought to be incompatible. As many have pointed out, the two-natures concept has often suppressed certain biblical themes which are central to the drama of salvation, namely, that God suffers, that God undergoes change for the sake of God's own fixed will to love. In other words, *some* dogma about the dual character of the person of Jesus was necessary and, once the language of "natures" was accepted into the inevitable dogmatic formulations, it was an easy step to fill those two natures with material which so defined the differences between the divine and the human that it was then regarded as impossible that God could experience what Scripture says Jesus experienced. Christology thus both protected and controlled soteriology and in turn rendered the experienced fact of Jesus as Savior unintelligible, at least for many contemporaries.

23. A quick review of the several theories of atonement would show that soteriology is a much more subtle form of theorizing and thus is resistant to any finished formula. Salvation is an event, a story to be told, a fact to be experienced. All the theories derive both their power and their weaknesses from their root metaphors which are essentially social and dramatic. Ransom, satisfaction, influence, victory, release, forgiveness, substitution—all are terms of social interaction, of dramatic narrative. By calling to mind various patterns of social organization or activity (marketplace, military life, law court, family, cult, or society) these terms make clear to the imagination what sort of change has taken place *between* God and the creatures *through* Jesus as Savior. All of the theories assume a need for salvation; where they differ is in the mechanics by which God in Jesus as Savior removes the threat of lostness and establishes a new relationship with the creatures who have, by their own misuse of creaturely freedom, put themselves in a condition of lostness from which they are not able to be rescued without the Savior come from God.

24. I take this to be the clear implication of Schillebeeckx's contention that ". . . the crisis lies in the fact that Jesus is still regularly explained to us as salvation and grace in terms which are no longer valid for our world of experience . . ." (Edward Schillebeeckx, *Christ: The Experience of Jesus as Lord* [New York: Seabury, 1980] p. 63).

25. My colleague, Professor Paul Sponheim, has helped me more than any other to appreciate the triadic character of theology implied by Christian faith. I have, most probably, done violence to Sponheim's elegant system by proposing my own version of triad in far more formal terms as a scheme by which to sift through the Christological proposals which cascade each month from the publishers. See his *Faith and Process: the Significance of Process Thought for Christian Faith* (Minneapolis: Augsburg, 1979).

26. See the discussion by W. Richard Comstock, "Toward Open Definitions in Religion," *Journal of the American Academy of Religion* 52 (September 1984): 499-517. The following from that essay is an expansion on what is intended by the assertion that "*how* one speaks of God, world, and self is an open

proposition today." Comstock writes, "An open definition is a process of continuous interrogation rather than a definitive answer provided in advance of the empirical investigation that it initiates. It is a point of departure, not a conclusion" (p. 510). One can claim this notion of "open definition" as a guiding principle for theology today, assuming, as most do, that theology has no privileged status among other disciplines, although its subject—as already noted—may be distinctively triadic. Again, Comstock: "There is no discipline from art to physics that knows the absolute boundaries of its concern. . . . An open definition is all that a scholar requires, since he needs to know how to begin, not where to end" (p. 514).

27. Readers of the work of Professor David Tracy of the University of Chicago will recognize some parallels between those theologians treated in Chapters 2, 3, and 4 and Tracy's distinction between theologies of proclamation, manifestation, and action. Whereas Tracy emphasizes primarily methodological issues, the emphasis in this study is on the material questions implied by the three basic questions. Chapter 5 has no clear parallel in Tracy. See David Tracy, *The Analogical Imagination: Christian Theology and the Culture of Pluralism* (New York: Crossroad, 1981). Similarly, there are parallels in this book to Tracy's discussion of the ordered relationships of God-Self-World, especially pp. 429ff.

Chapter Two: The Savior as the Word and as the End

1. Eberhard Busch, *Karl Barth: His Life from Letters and Autobiographical Texts* (Philadelphia: Fortress, 1975), p. 411.
2. From the German edition of Barth's lectures on 19th-century theology; cited by Helmut Gollwitzer, *Karl Barth: Church Dogmatics, A Selection with Introduction* (Edinburgh: T. & T. Clark, 1961), pp. 14f.
3. From Barth's post–World War II lectures at Bonn, published in English as *Dogmatics in Outline* (London: SCM, 1949), p. 59.
4. Karl Barth, *Protestant Thought: From Rousseau to Ritschl* (New York: Harper and Row, 1959), p. 316.
5. Ibid., p. 324.
6. See Busch, p. 246. The Ansbach Statement can be found in *Two Kingdoms, One World*, ed. Karl H. Hertz (Minneapolis: Augsburg, 1976), pp. 187ff.
7. Busch, p. 435.
8. *Dogmatics in Outline*, pp. 25f.
9. For example, see *Church Dogmatics* I. 1, *The Doctrine of the Word of God* (New York: Scribner, 1936), p. 227: "This point of contact is what theological anthropology, in correspondence with Gen. 1:27, calls the 'image of God' in man. But . . . the humanity and personality of sinful man simply cannot signify conformity with God, a point of contact with the Word of God . . . . The 'image of God' is not only, as we say, with the exception of some remnants ruined, but annihilated. . . . Man's capacity for God, however it may be with his humanity and personality, has been lost. We cannot, therefore, see that at this point there comes into view a common basis of discussion for philosophical and theological anthropology, the opportunity for a common exhibition at least of the possibility of raising the question about God." Barth is here rehearsing his famous dispute with Emil Brunner.

10. *Dogmatics in Outline,* p. 23.
11. *Church Dogmatics* I.2, p. 259.
12. Barth does not take up "salvation" as an explicit topic until vol. 4, and then "reconciliation" consumes 3000 pages. But the whole of the system presumes the God-human "meeting." God is the God who is absolutely free but who freely gives Godself to humanity in love.
13. See Barth on Ritschl in *Protestant Thought.*
14. Karl Barth, *Evangelical Theology: An Introduction* (New York: Holt, Rinehart, Winston, 1963), p. 15.
15. Ibid., p. 20.
16. Ibid., p. 35.
17. See especially Carl E. Braaten, *Christ and Counter-Christ: Apocalyptic Themes in Theology and Culture* (Phildelphia: Fortress, 1972), and *The Flaming Center: A Theology of the Christian Mission* (Philadelphia: Fortress, 1977). Particularly relevant for Moltmann's Christology are *The Crucified God* (New York: Harper and Row, 1974) and *The Trinity and the Kingdom* (San Francisco: Harper and Row, 1981), especially 3, "The History of the Son," and 4, "The World of the Trinity."
18. Published by Fortress. The influence of Frei's approach can be seen in Peter C. Hodgson, *Jesus—Word and Presence: An Essay in Christology* (Philadelphia: Fortress, 1971). See the explicit reference on p. xiv.
19. Published by Westminster: all remaining citations are from this volume.
20. Pp. 34, 25.
21. P. 35.
22. Pp. 47f.
23. For Pannenberg's argument for the probability of the historicality of the resurrection, see pp. 88-105.
24. P. 89.
25. P. 98.
26. P. 99.
27. P. 107.
28. P. 109.
29. P. 131.
30. P. 83.
31. Pp. 192f.
32. P. 84.
33. P. 85.
34. P. 205.

Chapter Three: The Savior as New Being and as Creative Transformation

1. Paul Tillich, *Systematic Theology* 1 (Chicago: University of Chicago Press, 1951), pp. 6f.
2. Paul Tillich, *Systematic Theology* 2 (Chicago: University of Chicago Press, 1957), pp. 138f. Citations will hereafter be designated as *S.T.*
3. *S.T.* 2: 146; emphasis added.
4. *S.T.* 2: 150f.
5. *S.T.* 2: 150.

6. *S.T.* 2: 151.
7. *S.T.* 2: 152.
8. This is obviously to claim that Tillich really wrote the first volume as a basis for a Christology that will meet the soteriological test. It is no surprise that his Christology is shaped subsequently by his ontology, and it can be debated whether it really serves or hinders proclamation. But the claim that Tillich really *intended* his Christology to be a viable representation of Jesus Christ as Savior is supported both by his own claims for the method in the introduction to volume 1 and elsewhere, and by his assertion that salvation is the criterion and the presupposition of every Christology.
9. *S.T.* 1: 9.
10. *S.T.* 2: 27.
11. *S.T.* 2: 24.
12. *S.T.* 2: 30.
13. Reinhold Niehbuhr, "Biblical Thought and Ontological Speculation in Tillich's Theology," in *The Theology of Paul Tillich*, ed. Charles W. Kegley and Robert W. Bretall (New York: Macmillan, 1952) pp. 216ff.
14. *S.T.* 2: 41ff.
15. *S.T.* 2: 44.
16. *S.T.* 2: 46.
17. Tillich here stands in the line of philosophers who argue that falsification of ontological structures is simply impossible. They never take a holiday, as Whitehead put it. Thus what one discovers by immediate self-knowledge must be assumed to be somehow characteristic of all beings whatsoever. See Langdon Gilkey, "The New Being and Christology," in *The Thought of Paul Tillich*, ed. James Luther Adams, Wilhelm Pauck, and Roger Lincoln Shinn (San Francisco: Harper, 1985), pp. 307-329. Tillich makes no absolute distinction between self and world, but he does make a sharp distinction between God and the world. For Tillich, God participates in the finite realm of self and world without God's unconditional freedom in any way being affected by that participation. When challenged by Charles Hartshorne on that point Tillich replied, "The justified religious interest in Mr. Hartshorne's concept of the divine finitude is much better safeguarded by Luther's symbolic statement that the intolerable 'naked absolute' makes himself small for us in Christ. In such a formula God's unconditional freedom is safeguarded in spite of his participation in finitude." Cf. "Reply to Interpretation and Criticism," in Kegley and Bretall, p. 340.
18. "Every systematic theology engages in more ontological speculation than does Biblical thought. The Bible conceives life as a drama in which human and divine actions create the dramatic whole. There are ontological presuppositions for this drama, but they are not spelled out." This is Niebuhr's acknowledgment of the theologian's obligation to speculate and argue for what the Bible assumes (in Kegley and Bretall, p. 216).
19. These themes are presented in *S.T.* 2, Part III, especially in the section entitled "Existential Self-destruction and the Doctrine of Evil."
20. Although lostness as estrangement is not based explicitly or exclusively on biblical revelation, it is in Tillich's thought primarily a theological, not a philosophical or sociological, idea. Thus it is derived from the reality of God. In

theology, talk about God takes priority over talk about sin, even though the two are inseparable. See, for example, "Sin and Evil," by Paul R. Sponheim, in *Christian Dogmatics*, vol. 1, ed. Carl E. Braaten and Robert W. Jenson (Philadelphia: Fortress, 1984): "While the concept of God can be adequately defined in principle apart from any reference to sin, the converse is not true. Sin is precisely, 'before God.' More precisely . . . against the will of God" (p. 363).

21. See the essays in Paul Tillich, *Theology of Culture*, ed. R. C. Kimbell (New York: Oxford University, 1959), e.g., "Protestantism and Artistic Style," "Aspects of a Religious Analysis of Culture," and "Existential Philosophy: Its Historical Meaning." See also essays in his honor in *Religion and Culture*, ed. Walter Leibrecht, who recalls, "In his lecture on 'The Theology of Culture' (1919), which made him well known in Europe overnight, [Tillich] speaks of the artist as the priest of the future church" (p. 7).

22. See *S.T.* 2: 168. Tillich abandons the traditional distinction between the person and the work of Christ. "It created the impression that the person of Christ is a reality in itself without relation to what has made him the Christ, namely, the New Being—the power of healing and salvation—in him."

23. *S.T.* 2:150f.

24. *S.T.* 2: 92.

25. Ibid.

26. *S.T.* 2: 98.

27. *S.T.* 2: 120f.

28. *S.T.* 2: 125.

29. *S.T.* 2: 47-55.

30. *S.T.* 2: 125ff.

31. *S.T.* 2: 134. The absence of estrangement in Jesus is not the only evidence of Jesus' unity with God. Already in volume 1 Tillich had identified Jesus as the final revelation of God in terms of Jesus' self-sacrifice. "A revelation is final if it has the power of negating itself without losing itself. . . . He who is the bearer of the final revelation must surrender his finitude . . . . In doing so, he affirms that he is the bearer of final revelation. . . . He becomes completely transparent to the mystery he reveals" (*S.T.* 1: 133).

32. *S.T.* 2: 134f.

33. *S.T* 2: 166.

34. Ibid.

35. *S.T.* 2: 167; emphasis added.

36. *S.T.* 2: 168.

37. *S.T.* 2: 176-180. Tillich closes his Christology by referring to the threefold character of salvation. (1) The New Being saves wherever one is grasped by the saving power of the New Being and thus participates in it: this is regeneration. (2) There can be no salvation unless it is accepted. "The cause is God alone . . . but the faith that one is accepted is the channel through which grace is mediated." This is justification. (3) "Sanctification is the process in which the power of the New Being transforms personality and community. . . ." Thus, although within history salvation remains relative, ambiguous, and hidden, Tillich argues that it is a reality whose manifestations, partial and relative though they be, are expressions of the New Being. The final volume is his rich and

intricate description of this reality, under the headings "Life in the Spirit" and "History and the Kingdom of God."

38. John B. Cobb Jr., *God and the World* (Philadelphia: Westminster, 1969), p. 126.
39. John B. Cobb Jr., *A Christian Natural Theology* (Philadelphia: Westminster, 1965), p. 266.
40. For Cobb's discussion of relativism in theology, see "Further Reflections on the Relativity of Belief," in *John Cobb's Theology in Process,* ed. David Ray Griffin and Thomas J. J. Altizer (Philadelphia: Westminster, 1977), pp. 165-170.
41. *God and the World,* p. 131.
42. Even in ordinary speech we are accustomed to interchanging seeing with interpreting. What one sees as the world is conditioned by how one interprets the process.
43. As in "Plurality and Its Theological Implications," a paper presented to the Hyde Park Ecumenical Project, March 8, 1985. The fact of religious pluralism relativizes every religious claim to finality or exclusivity, but, Gilkey points out, when one must take action, there is no guidance from relativism. Relativism immobilizes. Thus there is "the apparent contradiction between the requirement within political action for some fixed or absolute center and an equally unavoidable relativism." Gilkey argues for what he terms a "relative absolute," so that in Christian symbols "there is a relative manifestation of absolute meaning. They are true and yet relatively true; they represent a particularization of the absolute, and yet are relative and so only one manifestation."
44. *John Cobb's Theology in Process,* p. 158.
45. See John B. Cobb Jr., *Is It Too Late? A Theology of Ecology* (Beverly Hills: Bruce, 1972).
46. *God and the World,* p. 91.
47. Ibid., p. 89.
48. Ibid., p. 88.
49. Of course, the concern for the environment is not restricted to process theologians. See, for example, Joseph Sittler, *Essays on Nature and Grace* (Philadelphia: Fortress, 1972). Paul Santmire, *The Travail of Nature: The Ambiguous Promise of Christian Theology* (Philadelphia: Fortress, 1985). See also George Hendry, *Theology of Nature* (Philadelphia: Westminster, 1980), as well as Carl E. Braaten in the already-cited *Christ and Counter-Christ,* "Toward an Ecological Theology."
50. *Is It Too Late?* pp. 13-17.
51. John B. Cobb Jr., *Christ in a Pluralistic Age* (Philadelphia: Westminster, 1975), p. 182. See also Gordon Kaufman, *Theology for a Nuclear Age* (Philadelphia: Westminster, 1985), especially "Nuclear Eschatology."
52. Ibid., p. 183.
53. Ibid., p. 59.
54. Ibid., p. 187.
55. Ibid.
56. Ibid., p. 186.
57. Ibid.

58. Cobb is not alone among the process theologians in trying to show how the *intention* of orthodox doctrine concerning Christ's unity with the Father can be successfully sustained without continuing to use the conceptual language of the past. Cobb offers four criteria for any proposed image of Christ: (1) It must be recently "forged in the heat of the crosscurrents of contemporary thinking." (2) It must be open to reformulation and not "an image of a fixed condition of perfection." (3) To accept such an image must open one to be transformed in the present, rather than to be closed to the here and now. (4) The image must arise "through an encounter with Jesus' words or as a result of immersion in his field of force" (p. 188).

59. Since the appearance of *Christ in a Pluralistic Age*, Cobb has published two small books which have much in common with recent developments in Christology, some of which will be taken up in later chapters. Each of these books reflects a distinctive context for Christology. *Beyond Dialogue: Toward a Mutual Transformation of Christianity and Buddhism* (Philadelphia: Fortress, 1982) is a contribution to theology in the context of interreligious conversation. *Process Theology as Political Theology* (Philadelphia: Westminster, 1982) addresses the Christians' responsibility within the political context, an issue that is central to liberation, feminist, and black theologians.

Chapter Four: The Savior as Liberator and as Reconciler

1. Hugo Assmann, *Theologia desde la praxis de la liberacion* (1973), cited by Leonardo Boff, *Jesus Christ Liberator: A Critical Christology for Our Time* (Maryknoll, N.Y.: Orbis, 1981), p. 321.

2. Although most references in this section will be to Latin American theologians, the attempt here is to speak as broadly of liberation as possible, and thus to include, for example, the intention, if not the substance, of the work of women and blacks in the United States. Liberation theology is most certainly not one simple thing but it would be too awkward to qualify every reference to liberation theology with mention of Hispanics, women, and others.

3. John Hick, ed., *The Myth of God Incarnate* (Philadelphia: Westminster, 1977), and Don Cupitt, *The Debate about Christ* (London: SCM, 1979).

4. Gustavo Gutiérrez, *A Theology of Liberation: History, Politics and Salvation* (Maryknoll, N.Y.: Orbis, 1973), pp. 11f.

5. This is the major theme of Juan Luis Segundo, s.J., *Liberation of Theology* (Maryknoll, N.Y.: Orbis, 1976)

6. Gutiérrez, p. 15.

7. See articles by Robert McAfee Brown, Vine Deloria, Rosemary Ruether, and others in *Mission Trends No. 4: Liberation Theologies in North America and Europe*, ed. Anderson and Stransky (New York: Paulist, 1979).

8. In these chapters Cobb's Christology is a major example of significant reliance on a philosophical system. Other efforts are being made to develop the strengths of Hegel's Christology, even as there are reactions against such attempts. For instance, see American Academy of Religion Newsletter, *Currents in Contemporary Christology*, 1, Joseph Prabhu, "Hegel's Christology: A Mediation between Left- and Right-Hegelians," which includes a response to Rolf Ahlers' critical essay, "Hegel's Theological Atheism."

9. For a brief review of some of the significant literature on a Christian evaluation of both capitalism and Marxism see Jon P. Gunnemann, "Christian Ethics in a Capitalist Society," *Word and World* 5 (1985): 49-59.

10. Milan Machovec, *A Marxist Looks at Jesus* (Philadelphia: Fortress, 1972), with an introduction by Peter Hebblethwaite.

11. Juan Luis Segundo, *Faith and Ideologies* (Maryknoll, N.Y.: Orbis, 1984), p. 42. This is volume 1 of Segundo's *Jesus of Nazareth Yesterday and Today.*

12. Gutiérrez, p. 45.

13. Segundo, *Faith and Ideologies*, p. 42. Segundo's definitions of *faith* and *ideology* are rather idiosyncratic. He regards both as anthropological, and not exclusively theological, terms. Faith is the basic trust or the fundamental values by which one structures one's life. It is just there in human existence as such. Ideology, which can take the form of religion, although it implies faithlike reliance, refers more precisely to the technique or method upon which one depends as the means for accomplishing certain ends. It is nonvaluational about reality. Every "faith" employs "ideology" as a means. By adopting these definitions Segundo is then able to argue that it is legitimate for faith in the distinctively Christian sense to adopt the ideology of Marxism as the means to Christian ends.

14. It has sometimes been observed that liberation theologians are not helpful with questions plaguing many Christians in affluent societies. It is not clear from the view of liberation theology just what it means to seek the neighbor's well-being in complex questions like abortion or ecology; see, e.g., John B. Cobb Jr., *Process Theology as Political Theology* (Philadelphia: Westminster, 1982).

15. Boff, *Jesus Christ Liberator,* p. 20. Boff's own methodological priorities are set forth as follows: The human takes priority over the ecclesiastical; the utopian vision over the present facts; the critical over the dogmatic, the social over the personal, and orthopraxis over orthodoxy (cf. pp. 44ff.).

16. Gutiérrez, p. 175.

17. Ibid., p. 208.

18. Segundo is an important exception in many respects.

19. One is reminded here of Reinhold Niebuhr's version of neoorthodoxy, which was forged in large measure out of Niebuhr's experience as a pastor in Detroit during the labor struggles early in this century. It was his great achievement that he persuaded a entire generation of liberal Protestants that one can begin to have even the faintest understanding of the unfathomable woes which have overtaken humanity in modern times only by reading the signs of the times in light of a theological interpretation of sin or lostness. For a biographical description of Niebuhr's developing thought during the 1920s, see Richard Wightman Fox, *Reinhold Niebuhr: A Biography* (New York: Pantheon, 1985), especially Chapter 5, "Henry Ford Is America."

20. Rosemary Ruether's brief statement is a good summary: "For liberation theologians sin means not only alienation from God and personal brokenness of life, but also the structural evils of war, racism, sexism and economic exploitation which allow some people to dehumanize others" (*To Change the World: Christology and Cultural Criticism* [New York: Crossroad, 1981], p. 19).

21. Ruether (ibid., cf. pp. 57ff.) and others argue that there is no hope of removing the conditions of poverty and environmental exploitation so long as the system of social domination remains intact.

22. I am indebted to a colleague, Vitor Westhelle, for his unpublished paper, "Is Liberation Theology a New Natural Theology?" for this brief discussion of the metabolism of labor.

23. See Segundo's analysis of Marxism, especially the section, "The Faith of Science and Reason," pp. 88ff., in *Faith and Ideologies*.

24. See Elizabeth Schusslcr Fiorenza, *In Memory of Her: A Feminist Theological Reconstruction of Christian Origins* (New York: Crossroad, 1983), especially "The Basileia Vision of Jesus as the Praxis of Inclusive Wholeness," pp. 118ff., and "The Patriarchalization of Church and Ministry," pp. 288ff. Also, James H. Cone, *God of the Oppressed* (New York: Seabury, 1975), especially Chapter 6, "Who Is Jesus Christ for Us Today?"

25. Boff, pp. 238f. For a presentation of the argument for the claim that revolution is a real possibility, see Jose Miguez Bonino, *Doing Theology in a Revolutionary Situation* (Philadelphia: Fortress, 1975).

26. Boff, p. 64.

27. Ibid., pp. 67f.

28. Ibid., p. 71.

29. Ibid., p. 274.

30. Ibid., p. 74.

31. Ibid., pp. 78f.

32. Ibid., pp. 291f.

33. Ibid., p. 266.

34. Ibid., p. 294.

35. Jon Sobrino, *Christology at the Crossroads: A Latin American Approach* (Maryknoll, N.Y.: Orbis, 1978), especially Chapters 10 and 11.

36. Boff, p. 248.

37. Sobrino, *Christology*, p. 334.

38. Ibid., p. 335.

39. Ibid., p. 337.

40. Edward Schillebeeckx, *Christ: The Experience of Jesus as Lord* (New York: Seabury, 1980), p. 29.

41. Father Schillebeeckx was born in Belgium in 1914, the sixth of 14 children. He entered the Dominican Order and was ordained a priest in 1941, completing his theological studies at Louvain in 1943, the year he began teaching. After the war he pursued doctoral studies in Paris, and returned to teaching at Louvain in 1947, completing his dissertation in 1951, part of which was published as *The Sacramental Economy of Salvation,* followed in 1958 by his well-known *Christ: The Sacrament of the Encounter with God.* During the Second Vatican Council he was an advisor to the Dutch bishops, although not an official *peritus.* He has been in conversation with theologians (Pannenberg, Moltmann, Metz, and others) as well as with philosophers. The late 1960s and early 1970s were a time of intense study for him and about this time he became convinced that "a new understanding of soteriology, or theology of salvation, had to be articulated." See Robert Schreiter, "Edward Schillebeeckx, An Orientation to His Thought," in *The Schillebeeckx Reader,* ed. Robert Schreiter (New York: Crossroad, 1984).

42. *Christ: The Experience,* p. 64.

43. See Schreiter, "An Orientation," pp. 14ff., and John Macquarrie's review of *Christ: The Experience* in *Scottish Journal of Theology* 35, no. 3 (1982).
44. Schillebeeckx, *Christ: The Sacrament of the Encounter with God* (New York: Sheed and Ward, 1963).
45. In the first volume, *Jesus: An Experiment in Christology* (New York: Seabury, 1979), three of the four long parts comprise Schillebeeckx's analysis and evaluation of the modern exegetical studies of the Gospels, and only in Part Four does he take up the question "Who Do We Say That He Is?" A large portion of the second volume is given over to an investigation of the several Christologies of the New Testament apart from the Synoptics.
46. *Christ: The Experience*, p. 756. The internal quotations here are from H. Kuitert, whom Schillebeeckx is citing with approval.
47. Ibid., pp. 32f.
48. Ibid., p. 62.
49. Ibid., pp. 76f.
50. Ibid., pp. 78.
51. Schreiter, "An Orientation," p. 15.
52. Edward Schillebeeckx, *Interim Report on the Books Jesus and Christ* (New York: Crossroad, 1981), pp. 18f.
53. *Interim Report*, p. 11.
54. *Interim Report*, pp. 11f.; emphasis added.
55. *Christ: The Experience*, p. 731.
56. Ibid., p. 734.
57. Ibid., pp. 734-736.
58. Ibid., pp. 736-737.
59. Ibid., pp. 737-738.
60. Ibid., pp. 738-739.
61. Ibid., pp. 740-741.
62. Ibid., pp. 741-742.
63. Ibid., p. 743.
64. Ibid., p. 29; *Interim Report*, p. 9.
65. *Interim Report*, p. 3.
66. *Jesus*, p. 80.
67. Ibid., pp. 44-45.
68. Ibid., p. 56.
69. Schillebeeckx's account of the disciples' conversion to Jesus as the Christ can be summarized as follows. At the time of the crucifixion they all abandoned Jesus. Later, Peter, the one who had denied Jesus most vehemently, took the initiative to summon them together. Schillebeeckx postulates "that after Jesus' death Peter was the first (male) disciple to reach the point of 'conversion' and to resume 'following after Jesus', and then other disciples as well, on Peter's initiative. Peter is therefore the first Christian confessor to arrive at a Christological affirmation; by virtue of his conversion he takes the initiative in assembling [the others]." Those who gathered were, of course, first constituted as disciples by the initiative of Jesus and his proffer of salvation before his death. When they gathered after his death, they were returning to him, and in the process of reciprocal communication among the Twelve they encountered again the reality of the forgiveness of Jesus even for their desertion of him.

"In their experience here and now of 'returning to Jesus', in the renewal of their own life they encounter in the present the grace of Jesus' forgiving; in doing so they experience Jesus as the one who is alive. A dead man does not proffer forgiveness. A present fellowship with Jesus is thus restored." Belief in the resurrection is predicated on the experience of Jesus' forgiveness after his death; that is, if Jesus is still alive in the community he must have been raised from the dead, even though there is no New Testament account of anyone actually witnessing his rising from the tomb; the appearance stories and the empty tomb accounts are all based on the prior experienced fact of the presence of Jesus alive in the community of faith.

"The experience of having their cowardice and want of faith forgiven them, an experience further illumined by what they were able to remember of the general tenor of Jesus' life on earth, thus became the matrix in which faith in Jesus as the risen One was brought to birth. They all of a sudden 'saw' it" (*Jesus*, pp. 389-392).
70. See "Experience and Faith," in *Christliche Glaube in Moderne Gesellschaft* 24 (1978), p. 76.
71. *Jesus*, pp. 185f.
72. Ibid., p. 192.

Chapter Five: The Savior as Total Presence and as Mediator of God

1. Tom F. Driver, *Christ in a Changing World: Toward an Ethical Christology* (New York: Crossroad, 1981), p. 3.
2. Ibid., p. 23.
3. Ibid., p. 37.
4. Ibid., p. 54.
5. Ibid., p. 81.
6. Ibid., p. 56. For a different argument against Christocentric Christology, and in support of an evolutionary Christology, see Eugene TeSelle, *Christ in Context, Divine Purpose and Human Possibility* (Philadelphia: Fortress, 1975). TeSelle stresses the test of coherence in an evolutionary age more than the test of socioethical consequences. For the theme of this chapter, the following quotation is especially apt.
   The humanity of Jesus, although it is shaped by and attests to the Word, neither exhausts the Word nor is the sole means of access to it, for the Word is both knowable and efficacious elsewhere. The uniqueness of Jesus . . . will consist, then, in being the touchstone by which other responses are judged (p. 164).
7. Driver, p. 75.
8. Thomas J. J. Altizer, *Total Presence: The Language of Jesus and the Language of Today* (New York: Seabury, 1980). Altizer's *The Gospel of Christian Atheism* was one of the principal titles of the so-called God-is-dead theology.
9. Driver, p. 145.
10. Peter Steinfels writes, "There has been no shortage of books worried about 'individualism,' usually understood as simple selfishness." Indeed! In fact, his comment is part of a review of *Habits of the Heart: Individualism and Commitment in American Life* by Robert N. Bellah, Richard Madsen, William

Sullivan, Ann Swidler, and Steven M. Tipton (Berkeley: University of California Press, 1985). Cf. "Up from Individualism," *The New York Times Book Review*, April 14, 1985.

11. One easily accessible variation of this theory can be found in Robert Bellah's essay, "Religious Evolution," published in his *Beyond Belief: Essays on Religion in a Post-traditional World* (New York: Harper and Row, 1970), pp. 20-45. John Cobb likewise elaborates on Karl Jaspers' doctrine of the axial period in *The Structure of Christian Existence* (Philadelphia: Westminster, 1967); see especially Chapter 5, "Axial Existence."

12. Altizer, p. 62.

13. Ibid., p. 102.

14. Ibid., p. 4.

15. Ibid., p. 7.

16. Ibid., p. 48.

17. Ibid.

18. Ibid., p. 49.

19. Ibid., p. 99.

20. Ibid., p. 101.

21. Ibid., p. 44.

22. Ibid., p. 101.

23. Ibid., pp. 106f.

24. John Hick, "The New Map of the Universe of Faiths," in *God and the Universe of Faiths: Essays in Philosophy of Religion* (London: Macmillan, 1977), p. 139.

25. John Hick, "The Essence of Christianity," in *God and the Universe of Faiths,* p. 117.

26. John Hick, "The Copernican Revolution in Theology," in *God and the Universe of Faiths,* p. 131.

27. Paul Tillich, *Christianity and the Encounter of World Religions* (New York: Columbia University, 1963), pp. 77ff.

28. "The Essence of Christianity," p. 119.

29. "The New Map," p. 145. For the second citation see "Jesus and the World Religions," in *The Myth of God Incarnate* (Philadelphia: Westminster, 1977), p. 181.

30. For a very even-handed survey of the variety of Christian responses to the world religions see Paul Knitter, *No Other Name? A Critical Survey of Christian Attitudes toward World Religions* (Maryknoll, N.Y.: Orbis, 1985). He sets forth his own proposal for a theocentric Christology, discussed in this chapter, for consideration by the whole Christian community. "It must win greater approval from the 'sense of the faithful' before it can be called a valid Christian path" (p. xiv).

31. Included in *Christianity and Other Religions: Selected Readings,* ed. John Hick and Brian Hebblethwaite (Philadelphia: Fortress, 1980) pp. 81-82.

32. From *Theological Investigations* V (1966), included in Hick and Hebblethwaite, pp. 64-65.

33. "Christianity and the Non-Christian Religions," p. 79, in Hick and Hebblethwaite.

190 The Anonymous Christ

34. John B. Cobb Jr., *Beyond Dialogue: Toward a Mutual Transformation of Chris-
    tianity and Buddhism* (Philadelphia: Fortress, 1982).
35. Knitter, *No Other Name?* especially pp. 182ff.
36. Ibid., pp. 182-184. See also the relevant chapters on "classicist" and "his-
    torical" theories of truth.
37. "The Christian in a Religiously Plural World," in Hick and Hebblethwaite, p.
    98..   .
38. Ibid., pp. 105-106.
39. Ibid., p. 91.
40. For a description of "passing over" see John Dunne, *The Way of All the World*
    (New York: Macmillan, 1972). Cobb makes use of this notion in *Beyond
    Dialogue* (see Chapter 4, "Passing Over"), as does J. A. T. Robinson in *Truth
    Is Two-Eyed* (Philadelphia: Westminster, 1979), pp. 21ff., where he cites
    Dunne:

    > The holy man of our time, it seems, is not a figure like Gotama or Jesus
    > or Mohammed, a man who could found a world religion, but a figure like
    > Gandhi, a man who passes over by sympathetic understanding from his
    > own religion to other religions and comes back again with new insight to
    > his own. Passing over and coming back, it seems, is the spiritual adventure
    > of our time.

41. R. Panikkar, *The Intra-Religious Dialogue* (New York: Paulist, 1978), p. 54.

**Chapter Six: The Anonymous Christ: A Constructive Christology for
Postmodern Christians**

1. Few theologians neglect to make this point about the inestimable value of Greek
   philosophy for articulating and defending the faith. Carl E. Braaten states with
   characteristic vividness, "The church fathers worked with the only ontology
   they had at their disposal, transforming it to fit their biblical faith . . . . The
   use of Greek ontology was the *aggiornamento* of the church's theology in that
   time. . . . [But] the absolute God of Greek metaphysics was heartless, graceless
   and faceless. That God could not suffer, because suffering meant lack, and
   God does not lack anything. God must be beyond the pale of human suffering.
   God must be impassible, apathetic, and without compassion. The picture of
   Christ in the New Testament, by contrast, is full of suffering" (*Christian
   Dogmatics*, ed. Carl E. Braaten and Robert W. Jenson, 2 vols. [Philadelphia:
   Fortress, 1984] 1:531). Although Braaten would not accept the formulation
   "the Anonymous Christ," his own approach to the relation between Christology
   and soteriology is not far from that of this book. He writes that "the content
   of Christ's work and the degree of decisiveness available for that work is directly
   correlated to the perception of the human predicament" (p. 454).
2. This is the familiar distinction between *fides qua creditur* and *fides quae creditur.*
3. Cf. Wayne A. Meeks, *The First Urban Christians: The Social World of the
   Apostle Paul* (New Haven: Yale University Press, 1983). In spite of the fact
   that "a number of scholars, principally theologians, have warned that sociological interpretations of religious phenomena are inevitably reductionistic"
   (p. 2), there has been renewed interest in this approach to Scripture. Meeks's

study includes an extensive bibliography and points the reader to several brief histories of such scholarship.

4. See David Tracy, *The Analogical Imagination: Christian Theology and the Culture of Pluralism* (New York: Crossroad, 1981). For Tracy's description of the three "publics" of theology and his portraits of fundamental, systematic, and practical theologians see pp. 3-98. For his interpretation of contemporary Christologies see pp. 371-404. Cultural pluralism, for Tracy, includes a plurality of interpretations of the "situation," or of what I have called the perception of lostness. He writes of Tillich, for example: "For unlike the 'situation' in Tillich's period . . . our situation poses no one *dominant* question. Even the profound sense of meaninglessness, absurdity, the radical threat of nonbeing elicited by Tillich and his existentialist contemporaries as at the heart of his situation may now be viewed as one fundamental and permanent question . . ." (p. 341).

5. For example, see "The Gospel of Salvation and the World Religions" in Carl E. Braaten, *The Flaming Center: A Theology of the Christian Mission* (Philadelphia: Fortress, 1977).

6. See Langdon Gilkey, "The New Watershed in Theology," in *Society and the Sacred* (New York: Crossroad, 1981).

7. Gilkey, "Toward a Redefinition of Universal Salvation in Christ," in *Society and the Sacred*, p. 157.

8. See Chapter 2, note 1.

9. Gordon Kaufman, *Theology for a Nuclear Age* (Philadelphia: Westminster, 1985), p. 55. Kaufman has given much attention to the need for new images for God, most particularly in *Theological Imagination: Constructing the Concept of God* (Philadelphia: Westminster, 1981).

10. Kaufman, *Theology for a Nuclear Age*, p. 57.

DATE DUE